John Muir Summering in the Sierra

John Muir Summering in the Sierra

Edited by

Robert Engberg

University of Wisconsin Press

Published 1984

The University of Wisconsin Press
114 North Murray Street
Madison, Wisconsin 53715

The University of Wisconsin Press, Ltd.
1 Gower Street
London WC1E 6HA, England

First printing

Printed in the United States of America

For LC CIP information see the colophon

ISBN 0-299-09620-3 cloth; 0-299-09624-6 paper

To
SHERRY ENGBERG
This, John Muir's Book,
Is Dedicated

CONTENTS

ILLUSTRATIONS

ACKNOWLEDGMENTS

This book would not have been possible without the generous help of Ronald H. Limbaugh, archivist at the Holt-Atherton Pacific Center for Western Studies, who over the years has made the Muir Papers available to scholars; and of Dan Collins and Janich Magdich of the Center, who supplied copies of several *Evening Bulletin* letters. Thanks are also due to Ranger William H. Beat for supplying information about the local history of Mount Shasta, and to Mike and Maggie Rivers, Yosemite Institute instructors and National Park rangers at Glacier Bay, for leading me to think more deeply about Muir's place in contemporary thought. Staff members at the Bancroft Library, the State Historical Society of Wisconsin, and the library of the University of California, San Diego, were generous with their efforts, as was Mrs. Elaine Brunton, librarian and colleague. Thanks also to Michael Cohen, David Lester, Professor John E. Ross, and Elizabeth Steinberg for useful criticisms of the Introduction. Special help was given by my friend Donald Wesling of John Muir College. Douglas Haller of the California Historical Society and friend Bert Kersey aided in illustrating this book. My students—and most especially those who have joined me in study-tours at Yosemite Valley—have influenced this book's making more than they know. My thanks also go to Brian Keeling, my editor at the University of Wisconsin Press, for working so arduously to make this a better volume—one worthy of the Press and of Muir. As always, love and thanks go to my sister Marilyn, and to my wife Sherry and our children Brock and Catherine, for letting me spend the necessary hours away from them in order to complete this work.

PREFACE

This book consists of articles written by John Muir for the San Francisco *Daily Evening Bulletin* in the years 1874–1875. Coming after the extended period when Muir lived in the Yosemite Valley—years when he formed his wilderness ethic—these letters may be read as a continuation of his autobiography, taking his story from the moment he walks out of Yosemite to the time his travels encompass nearly the whole of California. As eye-witness accounts of the 1870s, these letter-articles are also valuable enlargements of earlier observations made by William Brewer in his *Up and Down California in 1860–1864* and by Clarence King in *Mountaineering in the Sierra Nevada*.

John Muir sent down from the mountains of California both an invitation and a warning. Telling his readers "to climb the mountains and get their good tidings," he also insisted they become stewards of the earth. At the very moment in the state's history when "materialism ruled supreme," he challenged the frontier view of landscape as a resource made for man. Muir sought to enlighten his readers with his own mountain experience, and in these articles directed to the *Bulletin*—but which in reality are letters addressed to civilization—he asked his readers to see, hear, and believe in a radically new way.

Muir invented a new ethics-centered type of reporting, "wilderness journalism," to spread his message. Composed in the field and sent to the publisher without later revisions and redrafting, it retains the freshness and spontaneity that characterize Muir's best writing. These contributions to the *Evening Bulletin*—many reprinted here for the first time in over a century—are in fact accounts of both the observed and the observer. Behind every report about people and places lies Muir's own story of why he quit his solitary wanderings to become the leader of the American conservation movement.

San Diego   R.E.
June 1983

John Muir Summering in the Sierra

INTRODUCTION
Wilderness Journalism

> Bless me, what an awful thing town
> duty is! I was once free as any pine-
> playing wind, and feel that I have still
> a good length of line, but alack! there
> seems to be a hook or two of civiliza-
> tion in me that I would fain pull out,
> yet *would not pull out*—O, O, O!!!
> Muir to Mrs. Ezra S. Carr,
> July 31, 1875

> Longest is the life that contains the
> largest amount of time-effacing en-
> joyment; of work that is a steady de-
> light. Such a life may really comprise
> an eternity upon the earth.
> Muir to William Frederic Badè,
> 1914

John Muir was born in Dunbar, Scotland, in 1838. At the age of
ten he emigrated to Wisconsin, where he worked on the family
farm and stole what "precious moments" he could for study. A
chance to show some wooden inventions at the state fair led to
three years of study at the University of Wisconsin. He quit the
school in 1863 to begin the adventures which would lead him five
years later to his personal discovery of California's Yosemite
Valley. Here he dropped out of sight for several years, meeting a
few luminaries like Ralph Waldo Emerson but for the most part
lost in private study and reflection. He tried his hand at writing a
few articles, but had his first piece published anonymously and
the others forwarded to publishers by his friend and mentor
Mrs. Ezra Carr. In 1874 Muir left the Valley for the trips up and

3

"Mount Shasta." Engraver unknown. Ca. 1876. Courtesy the California Historical Society, San Francisco.

down California which are the subjects of the letter-articles in this book. In 1879 came the first of his adventures to Alaska's Glacier Bay, to be followed by his careers in farming and writing.

Sometime during the summer of 1871, while Muir was still working as a guide and amateur scientist in Yosemite, he received a small book entitled *The Growth of the Mind,* written by a Boston transcendentalist and preacher named Sampson Reed. Emerson mailed the book to Muir soon after the pair spent their memorable week together in Yosemite, and while he read the book Muir marked with a pencil the passages that particularly caught his eye. One sentence Muir noted was: "In books, science is presented to the eye of the pupil, as if it were [in a] dried and preserved state; the time may come when the instructor will take him by the hand, and lead him by the running streams, and teach him the principles of science as she comes from her Maker, as he would smell the fragrance of the rose without gathering it."[1] Young Muir found "much of the fountain truth" in Reed's writing. Here was justification for precisely the type of freedom he was enjoying and here was the method of experiential learning preached by Emerson. Here too was the implicit notion that science—indeed all knowledge—is to be shared.

Two opposing notions were troubling Muir while he lived in the Yosemite. He wondered whether he should lead others to the truths he was learning while a student in the "University of the Wilderness" (and if so then how best to show the way) or, on the other hand, remain quiet, holding his life and thoughts private, pure, and absolutely separate from the affairs of mankind. In one letter written at this time, Muir noted how difficult it would be to teach about so grand a subject as nature: "These mountain fires that glow in one's blood are free to all," he wrote to Mrs. Carr, "but I cannot find the chemistry that may press them unimpaired into booksellers' bricks."[2] For several years Muir confided his ideas in notebooks and journals. He jealously guarded

1. Sampson Reed, *The Growth of the Mind,* in the John Muir Papers, Holt-Atherton Pacific Center for Western Studies, University of the Pacific, Stockton, California.

2. William Frederic Badè, *Life and Letters of John Muir,* 2 vols. (Boston: Houghton Mifflin, 1923–24), 2:7.

the freedom of his Yosemite explorations and told Carr and others that only his geological research was important: "I will seek to be true to them," he said of his studies on the origins of the Valley, "although all the rest of the world of beauty besides these mountains burn and nebulize back to star smoke."[3] The first break in his self-imposed silence came in a letter written a few weeks after Emerson's visit. Should he hold his *wheesht* (the Scotch word for "silence")? Muir asked Mrs. Carr. The question was rhetorical: Muir knew the answer even as he asked it. He would abandon isolation. The choice was not easy, however, and he admitted in a later note that "book-making frightens me, because it demands so much artificialness and retrograding. . . . I find that though I have a few thoughts entangled in the fibres of my mind, I possess no words into which I can shape them."[4]

When Muir made the decision to write out what he had learned, he chose as one vehicle for his public statements the San Francisco *Daily Evening Bulletin.*[5] As a result of these writings, he quickly won modest notoriety as a naturalist with unconventional views about geology (theories which put him into direct conflict with authorities such as Josiah Whitney and Clarence King); then later, as his popularity spread, he was welcomed throughout the state as a lecturer known for an easy manner and earnest enthusiasm. When his articles began appearing in *Harper's* and the *Atlantic* he gained a national reputation as the chief naturalist of the giant sequoia, and at the century's turn he was recognized as this nation's chief spokesman for conservation. Writing his autobiography at age seventy, Muir said that his conservation efforts had gone mostly unheeded, and that the years spent at policy making had seen no "compelling interest or change in public opinion."[6] Nonetheless, by 1914, the year of

3. Jeanne C. Carr, "John Muir," *The Californian* 1 (1890): 94.

4. Badè, *Life and Letters,* 2:6.

5. The San Francisco *Daily Evening Bulletin* was founded in 1855 by James King of William (*né* James King), and its early, stormy history was marked by bitter antagonisms with the state's political machines and with rival editors, one of whom shot King to death on the steps of the newspaper's office. By 1874 the paper was four pages in length and eight columns wide, and had bold headings for its feature articles.

6. "Pelican Bay Manuscript," typescript copy page 211, John Muir Papers.

Muir's death, conservation was a national political force to be reckoned with, precisely because Muir had made it so.

When Muir made his commitment "to entice people to look at nature's loveliness" and began to write the letter-articles which appear in this book, he recognized that the West was losing the very promise which had first brought people to it. Muir taught himself to sense this change, to record it and to make it known to his generation. His insight came as the natural consequence of self-knowledge. He knew how his own relations with landscape had evolved, and this allowed him to see by way of contrast the relationship between other Americans and the land. His own experiences—his walk to Florida and his hike to Yosemite, his first summer in the Sierra and his climb of Mount Ritter—came to him while westerners were becoming more alienated from their environment. And so Muir sought to correct this direction, to free his countrymen from their myopic and "arithmetical" judgments, to bring mankind and mountain together.

The view of the world Muir gained while an ecstatic student of the wilderness, and the one he wished to share throughout his life and in his writings, had much in common with the world view of Eastern philosophy which became respectable only during Muir's lifetime. When Eastern mysticism enjoyed a fresh vogue again almost a century later, in the 1960s, the kernel idea that became a popular key to understanding was that of Yin and Yang. Essentially, this philosophy casts the earth as a universe of opposites, playing out its drama in unifying tension, with both life and death, light and dark, required for completeness. Muir's upbringing in a family that remained unified despite intense psychological warfare between the father and sons might have set the stage, psychologically, for his formal philosophical recognition that unity could subsist amidst the clash of opposing forces. More directly, he may have been helped along in this "enlightenment"[7] by some readings of the Oriental philoso-

7. The special sense of "enlightenment" I have in mind, which might be summed up as an intellectual and emotional comprehension of the world as a unified whole, is described by Thomas J. Lyon in "John Muir's Enlightenment," in Lawrence R. Murphy, ed., *The World of John Muir* (Stockton: The Holt-Atherton Pacific Center for Western Studies, 1981), pp. 51–57.

phies. We know, for example, that when living in Yosemite he was given some "Asiatic Sayings" by Mrs. Carr. Muir was reading Thoreau while in Yosemite, and of course he knew Emerson (whom he had met in 1870), as well as the thinking of lesser-known transcendentalists like Reed. But while indebted to others, he arrived at his own version of transcendentalism largely by intuition and meditation. He continued to distrust books as being separate from the realities of experience, calling them poor "piles of stone set up to show coming travelers where other minds have been."[8] The best activity was to "stand in what all the world would call an idle manner. . . . So-called sentimental, transcendental dreaming seems the only sensible and substantial business that one can engage in."[9]

To all outward appearances, Muir's life was anything but "idle," full of inactive "dreaming." His understanding of the world was achieved not by a reflectiveness entirely detached from experience, but by active engagement with the world. During his Yosemite years, for example, he pursued with relentless physical energy the puzzle of the Valley's glacial origin, a study that entailed mounting rugged peaks and exploring remote *Bergschrund* glacial wombs. During his writing of the articles that appear in this collection, Muir was in a constant motion that often seemingly left the "self" behind. He found no paradox in this apparent crazy divorce of body and psyche: "No sane man in the hands of Nature," he once wrote, "can doubt the doubleness of his life. Soul and body receive separate nourishment and separate exercise, and speedily reach a stage of development wherein each is known apart from the other. Living artificially, we seldom see much of our real selves."[10] The end result of these periodic divisions seems not to have been a schizophrenic breaking but rather a holistic gathering of mind and body. Muir often spoke of the numerous times he was connected to his surroundings and a part of them—the outcome of days spent enraptured

8. Linnie Marsh Wolfe, ed., *John of the Mountains: The Unpublished Journals of John Muir* (Boston: Houghton Mifflin, 1938), pp. 94–95.

9. Robert Engberg and Donald Wesling, eds., *John Muir to Yosemite and Beyond* (Madison: University of Wisconsin Press, 1980), pp. 87–88.

10. John Muir, "Explorations of the Great Tuolumne Cañon," *Overland Monthly* 11 (September 1873): 144.

in the study of rocks and granite and ice, and of nights when he "dreamed of glaciers" and planned his next day's travels. His ego and world became one, tied together with mystical threads created during those times when he was "as close to the heart of

A Self-Portrait. Drawing in a letter to Miss Janet Douglass Moores, February 23, 1887. Published in Badè, *Life and Letters,* vol. 1, between pp. 216–17. Courtesy the Bancroft Library.

the world" as he could be. Of the many records Muir left of this
discovery, perhaps none is more clearly stated than that in the
journal of his first summer in the Sierra: "No pain here, no dull
empty hours, no fear of the past, no fear of the future. These
blessed mountains are so compactly filled with God's beauty, no
petty personal hope or experience has room to be."[11]

Readers of the letter-articles in this volume may sense the difficulties Muir faced in distilling for the public what he knew.
Muir had come to believe that we must protect the land. He
viewed the mountain experience as one path to being "born
again." Nature could be a source of salvation no less than is
God—because Nature is God. These radical thoughts Muir expressed in convoluted ways one may well misunderstand if not
attentive. No doubt Muir's genuinely shy nature also hindered
his public expressions. He complained of becoming physically ill
before lecturing and often compared the task of writing to the
progress of a glacier—"one eternal grind." But despite their
shortcomings, these "Stormy Sermons" (as the best of his modern biographers, Michael Cohen, has termed them[12]) nonetheless
remain among the finest of Muir's autobiographical writings.
The literary self-effacement that arose from Muir's pointed attempt to make nature the central character in his articles is less
advanced here than later in his career. Also fortunately absent
from these early articles are some of the stylistic refinements of
his late writings, refinements that would make him a more polished writer but at a sacrifice of the immediacy which both
marks his greatest writing and best reveals his life. This particularly seems to have been the case with his last books: few would
disagree that *Our National Parks* (1901) or *The Yosemite* (1912),
while perhaps more stylistically "correct" than his earlier
works, were less inspired. (That his best book, *My First Summer
in the Sierra,* appeared in 1909 should not mislead: it is based on
the two notebooks of 1869.) If we are to know Muir's private
world, we must remind ourselves of its profound spirituality and
return to his earliest writings. This means going back to his note-

11. Quoted in Lyon, "John Muir's Enlightenment," p. 51.
12. See Michael Cohen, "Stormy Sermons," in *The World of John Muir,* ed.
Lawrence R. Murphy, pp. 21–36.

books and journals and, as we do in this book, to the unrevised newspaper articles of the *Evening Bulletin*.

Despite Muir's complaints about the "defrauding duties" imposed upon writers, and his constant wariness of words as a substitute for action, he sought to share his understanding of nature precisely through the written word. He assumed this literary role by listing himself in the 1876 *San Francisco Directory* as "Muir, John author *dwl* 1419 Taylor." Thus he established an address and a vocation. (The third important symbol of community living, his marriage, followed in 1880.) He often spoke to friends and interviewers during this time about his desire to quit the literary duties which bound him. But the frequent protestations that "town fog" choked him, and the playful boast that he could at a moment's notice "hop over the back fence" and be gone to the mountains, were in reality empty wishes. Muir simply could not allow himself to remain divorced from society. Many of his writings in the present book reveal why he could not.

The letter-articles from Muir's trips up and down California employ a style of reporting which was essentially another one of his inventions—wilderness journalism. This writing is always faithful to the author's observations, always attuned to his own vision of the earth, and has one central theme playing continuously throughout: the image of an "Earth planet-Universe" home as a whole whose parts interplayed continuously and harmoniously. To understand this play among life's forces demanded that Muir assume an active role in them, or as he said it, to be not *on* the earth but rather *in* it. So he became involved with the planet in an "enlightened" way, keeping himself in constant touch with the mountains while also reaching out to his community. His visits to cities increased, he made friends with other writers and with social activists like State Superintendent of Schools John Swett and the Carrs and the radical reformer Henry George; he joined the growing intellectual community forming around the new state university in Berkeley and began lecturing around the state. And, of course, he wrote to urge others to view land as their larger home: "The contemplation of a beautiful landscape excites the highest spiritual pleasure in us

... and most of the *real* real-estate of the world is of this eternal beauty sort, too often held of no account."[13]

By the mid-1870s Muir's concerns went a step farther beyond self-growth, obliging him to leave the comfortable but private Yosemite experience of solitary wandering and rumination. The leave-taking was a supremely important and absolutely necessary moment in his life. "No one of the rocks seems to call me now," he wrote to Carr in the fall of 1874, "nor any of the distant mountains. Surely this Merced and Tuolumne chapter of my life is done."[14] Thus Muir decisively dropped his former role as the ecstatic recluse in Yosemite to enter, however hesitantly, the social and political affairs of his community. His self-imposed task was now to make Californians know the pleasures of a mountain visit, and then (after gaining their confidence) to make city dwellers learn the "truth" of rock and tree, later even bringing some people together into a club—which would become national in scope—to advance conservation issues and combat the materialists in the legislative arena.

The biographer of John Muir is easily lured into picturing Muir as a seer who submitted to various stages of "preparation" for the noteworthy undertakings of his mature years—stages that were conceived, presumably, by some cosmic intelligence. Muir himself seemed on at least one occasion to encourage this view by endorsing Thoreau's belief that "we sit into as many dangers as we run into . . . we are carried and kept alive by a thousand miracles."[15] In fact, Muir's life reveals itself to have been as shaped by happenstance as any life; and the momentous decision he gradually made to mix hard politics with the mysticism of his youth, the choice that allowed him to become a social critic and political activist of exceptional power, appears to have hung in the balance for many years.

Details of how Muir became the *Evening Bulletin*'s correspondent are not clear. It seems unlikely that he initiated the contact

13. Quoted in *John Muir to Yosemite and Beyond,* ed. Robert Engberg and Donald Wesling, p. 8.

14. Letter to Mrs. Carr (September 1874), quoted in *John Muir to Yosemite and Beyond,* ed. Robert Engberg and Donald Wesling, p. 155.

15. "Pelican Bay Manuscript," typescript copy page 211, John Muir Papers.

Daily Evening Bulletin.

THURSDAY EVENING, JULY 20, 1876.

SUMMERING IN THE SIERRA.

John Muir Shakes the Dust of the Town from his Feet and Flees to the Mountains.

The Calaveras Grove—Some Facts About the Sequoia System.

[SPECIAL CORRESPONDENCE OF THE BULLETIN.]

BIG TREE GROVE, July 13, 1876.

Ho, weary town worker, come to the woods and rest ! I wish it were possible to compel all to come ; not that I am just at this moment seized with a fit of Quixotic philanthropy, for with Thoreau, I am convinced that the profession of doing good is full. It is hard, however, to see so many of the best of one's fellow-beings diseased with duties when Nature's rest-cure is so specific and available. Californians are not lazy ; on the contrary, we work too much and rest too little, hoping all the while in a vague way to escape the deplorable results. There is something inexpressibly mean in arithmetical arguments. They have the advantage, however, of being clear-edged and universally appreciable. I will therefore venture to offer the following :

THE UTILITY OF REST.

Rest pays even in a pecuniary way, for one will do more and better work in a lifetime by taking a good summer Sabbath every year : and those Sabbath months, in the total length of one's life, will rather be added, with good compound interest, at the end.

Opening Paragraphs of an Article by John Muir in the July 20, 1876, San Francisco *Daily Evening Bulletin*.

or applied for the position. More likely, Mrs. Carr, a friend of Benjamin Avery (editor of the *Overland Monthly* and one-time writer for the *Bulletin*), was responsible in some way for giving Muir the opportunity, perhaps introducing him to *Bulletin* editor Samuel Williams. In any event, when the *Overland* ceased publication in 1874, Muir had cause to find a new market for his manuscripts. The understanding seems to have been that Muir would be a "special correspondent" for the newspaper and would submit feature-length articles throughout the fall–winter and perhaps during the following summer. These letter-articles, as Muir called them, would be composed in the field and mailed to the *Bulletin* whenever he had the chance to do so. This meant that there would be little chance for revision of the articles, and indeed most appear to be first drafts composed either during his camping experiences or written immediately afterwards based on notes and journal entries. The *Bulletin* placed the first of Muir's contributions on the front page of its Thursday, October 29, 1874, edition, prominently displayed with a heading announcing "John Muir—the Naturalist . . ." as its author. Muir, aged thirty-six, was by this time known to San Franciscans through his articles in the *Overland Monthly*. But if he enjoyed a California readership from the monthly magazine, it was by necessity a limited one. Fewer than 3,000 copies of the *Overland* were published, and many of these went east on the new transcontinental railway. Readers fortunate enough to receive a copy belonged to the Bay Area's professional and literate classes; the *Bulletin,* by contrast, would be read by the local worker and by the growing middle class, precisely the group Muir believed worked too hard and most needed the benefits of mountain travel.

This book contains the first fifteen *Bulletin* articles written by Muir, dated from October 29, 1874, to November 18, 1875. Each describes a trip into a particular section of California's Mount Shasta or Sierra Nevada region. (Muir was to write later articles for the newspaper, but these are omitted here; they describe adventures outside California or beyond the theme of this book.) Muir probably did not title his letters, and the elaborate tiered headings they carried—omitted here except for main titles

—were no doubt added by the *Bulletin*'s editor. As an aid to modern readers, various typographical errors which crept into the *Bulletin*'s version of the letters have been corrected, though Muir's (occasionally inconsistent) choice of words and spellings has been kept: *cañon, canyon, bowlder, plashing.* Footnotes identify persons mentioned in the letters. Some figures, like artist William Keith and Shasta pioneer Justin Sisson, may be familiar to readers of California history. Others will not be known. But one of the charming aspects of the writings is the many unknown or forgotten personalities whom Muir met and included in his accounts, men like "Bloody Joe" Boler of Mono Lake, and John Nelder, who made his home in a sequoia grove. Places have changed over the century since Muir visited them, and his descriptions of Mono Lake, Kings Canyon, Yosemite, Shasta, and the town of "Sisson's" (now Mount Shasta City) contrast sharply with their present appearances. Certain botanical classifications have changed too, and, where helpful, present-day scientific as well as common names are supplied in footnotes. Introductory passages for each part and each article are intended to provide necessary background.

These letters may be read both as a continuation of Muir's autobiography and as a record of his entrance into society. If Muir longed for the simplicity and freedom which are so joyously present in the articles found in this volume, he knew it was also the historic moment for him to speak out in defense of the mountains. Muir's private wanderings of his Yosemite years ended with the publication of these letters. The years of public life and political debate, of book making and conservation battles won and lost, were beginning.

PART ONE
Mount Shasta and the Lava Beds

Come all who need rest and light,
bending and breaking with over
work, leave your profits and losses
and metallic dividends and come a
beeing.

December 17, 1874

When John Muir set out from Yosemite Valley in 1874 to head in
the northerly direction he called "Shastaward," he began also to do
the thing he claimed to hate most: the awful, tedious, "glacial" work
of public writing. He would have preferred the life of the solitary
mountaineer, left alone to his climbs and studies. Yet he had con-
tracted sometime during that summer or fall of 1874 to set down his
experiences and discoveries for the San Francisco *Daily Evening
Bulletin,* and this meant an inevitable loss of privacy. "I don't write
regularly for anything," he told his sister Sarah, "although I'm said
to be a regular correspondent of the *Evening Bulletin,* and have the
privilege of writing for it when I like."[1]

Muir began a journey that would take him during the next two
seasons on ever-widening travels into California's Shasta, Yosemite,
and Kings-Kaweah regions. These journeys totalled 4,000 miles, more
than half of which he would travel on foot. Muir lingered several
days at Lake Tahoe. Then in early October, 1874, he crossed the
Sierra to follow the California-Oregon stagecoach road north some
two hundred miles to a spot near the junction of the Pit, McCloud,
and Sacramento rivers. Here he rested a week at the new McCloud
River Salmon Hatchery, and here he wrote his first *Bulletin* article.

The hatchery had been founded two years before, and Muir's
account of it was probably the first published description of the place

1. Badè, *Life and Letters,* 2:63.

17

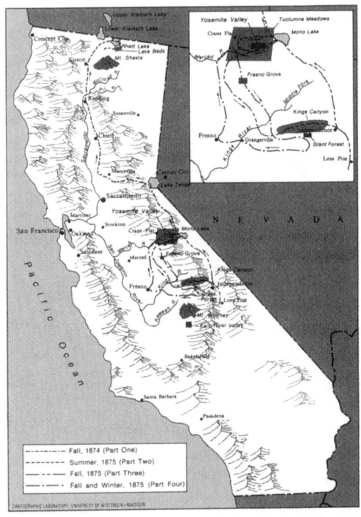

Muir's Travels in the Mount Shasta Area and the Sierra Nevada, October 1874–
November 1875.

known as the "U.S. Salmon-Breeding Establishment." Behind Muir's straightforward report on the hatchery's conservation techniques, active curiosity and some admiration for the ingeniousness of the system are evident. Modern readers will notice, too, that Muir shows a somewhat limited awareness of the ecological imbalance created by introducing alien species into an ecosystem; but it should be added in Muir's defense that, if he did not publicly raise the question of what effects the planting of eastern fishes into California streams might have, neither did anyone else at the time.

The purpose of the hatchery was to restock northern California rivers, recently decimated by the silt pollution of the hydraulic mines, with species of eastern fish, and to explore the possibility that native Chinook salmon might be exported to the East. Muir was evidently not convinced by the fish commissioner's argument that hatcheries were required because nature is "too slow," and he poked fun at the economics behind the "fishy" hatchery; he thought it ridiculous that California should have to pay for fingerlings whose parent-fish had been removed from the very streams into which the young fish were freed! And yet Muir was obviously interested in the still novel idea that wildlife might be raised in captivity and later released into the wilderness.

It was at the McCloud river that Muir made his first sustained contact with Native Americans. In his walks along the area's streams he was often accompanied by an Indian boy whom he called a "bright, inquisitive fellow"; the ten-year old impressed Muir with the local tribe's various crafts and skills, and Muir liked his knowledge and presence. (Muir once confessed he "rushed suddenly upon" the young Wintus, who nonetheless remained calm, shouting "Me no 'fraid; me Modoc.") The account is condescending, but genuinely sympathetic, and therefore unique in the literature of the time. Most white visitors to the region had been less generous in their judgments: William Brewer passed through the area a decade before and concluded the Wintus were "a very low, brutal-looking race"; Clarence King thought them "picturesque" yet was "almost afraid to describe the squalor and grotesque hideousness" of their condition.[3] Aside

2. Quoted in John Muir, *Picturesque California* (Boston: Deming, 1888), p. 201.

3. Francis P. Farquhar, ed., *Up and Down California in 1860-1864: The Journal of William H. Brewer* (1930; Berkeley: University of California Press, 1966), p. 301; Clarence King, *Mountaineering in the Sierra Nevada* (1872; Lincoln: University of Nebraska Press, 1970), p. 226. Brewer, a Yale graduate, linked up with the California State Geological Survey Party and spent four years exploring the state's mountains with Josiah Whitney and Clarence King.

from Muir, only Livingston Stone, the commissioner of the hatchery, had found beauty in the tribe's culture. In his report to the U.S. Fish Commission, Stone praised the honesty and high ethics of the Native "McCloud Indians," adding in a poignant note they were "not too proud to say to the white stranger, 'These are my lands,' and 'These are my salmon.'" Muir undoubtedly wished to find and describe in the tribe a type of pure primitivism to which he might call attention, and to draw from them a human example of the superiority of wilderness over civilization. But these apparently impoverished northern California Indians could not inspire him, and instead in his letter to the *Bulletin* he allowed only that the McCloud group had "better features" than the "Diggers" he had previously seen in and around the foothills of Yosemite. Later that winter, when Muir visited the lava beds of northeastern Shasta, the ancestral home of the Modocs, he would call for sympathy for the white soldiers who had been killed while carrying out their orders. It was not until his travels in Alaska that Muir found Indian cultures free from the compromising influences of civilization—cultures that he believed lived close enough to nature to have kept their natural, and hence superior, ways of life.

"Salmon-Breeding" is the first of five articles which Muir was to write from the Shasta and Modoc regions. It is found in the *Bulletin* of October 29, 1874, prominently headed on the front page.

Salmon-Breeding

ESCAPING TO THE MOUNTAINS

Icy Shasta[4] is a noble mark for a mountaineer, and I may soon reach it. Glaciers and pine-trees are in all my thoughts, but just at this moment they are decidedly fishy, a fact readily explainable by my contact with Commissioner Stone and his schools of McCloud river salmon. I was called upon to undergo some of the more characteristic of the processes and vicissitudes of civili-

4. Mount Shasta, elevation 14,162', is the largest of the Cascade Range volcanoes. It last erupted some 200 years ago, although it is still considered to be active. Clarence King discovered glaciers on the northern flank of the mountain in 1870; five small, residual glaciers remain near the crest, and their presence was one deciding factor in bringing Muir to the area. The volcanic plug on Shasta's western flank now known as Black Butte was once called "Muir's Peak," and is so identified in many old photographs.

zation through a period of three hundred days, beginning in the November mists of 1873, and ending with the first ripe golden-rods of 1874. At the close of this season of fog and refinement I fortunately made good my escape to the mountains, proceeding up the Merced to Yosemite, thence across the summit, through Bloody Canyon Pass, and along the eastern base of the range, over the wide basins and valleys of the Mono, Walker, and Carson; thence up into the lake district of Donner and Tahoe, and northward toward icy Shasta. But Shasta's white cone is still eighty miles away, and I have made no advancement for a week, being caught and scholared in the fish schools of the Commissioners. It is stormy now, but the weather was calm a week ago, and I winnowed my way through the weeds and bushes of the foot-hills softly as a salmon in deep waters. Most of the summer flowers are dead, but interesting work was easily found in comparing the pines, and the rock forms and general aspects of these Shasta hills with those of corresponding position and elevation in the southern portion of the range. The discovery of a new species of woodpecker and three new species of eriogonum,[5] to-gether with a finely fruited and finely colored wild grape-vine that I had never met before made my first day in this region especially joyous, and, of course, night overtook me ere I was aware. A teamster, into whose good graces I found my way by telling a Bret Harte story, directed me to "Allen's," half a mile above this place, where I was assured of finding food and a bed.[6] It was late in the afternoon when I crossed the Pitt river, and dusky twilight was stealing over all the landscape when I reached the banks of the McCloud. The fire of an Indian encampment blazed on a hill to my left, while in front and close to the water's edge I caught sight of a broad expanse of white canvas, which at first appeared to be a shining pool belonging to the river, but on being approached closely, proved to be a large tent with a pair of small pine cabins by its side; and from a tall pole in front the stars and stripes were emphatically displayed.

At Allen's I lost no time in making inquiries concerning the strange camp, and was gladly surprised to learn that it was the

5. Wild buckwheat.
6. "Allen's," or "Allen's Station," is now under a bay of Shasta Lake.

McCloud Salmon-egg establishment, and that Stone himself was present. Hastening back next morning, I was received with genuine kindness by the Commissioner, who at once began to initiate me into the workings of the establishment, and moreover promised to accompany me on my excursion to Mt. Shasta, provided I would wait a few days until he could make the necessary arrangements. Fortunately, the season's work was well nigh completed—the last installment of eggs were being packed for shipment, when he would be entirely free. Livingston Stone[7] has long been known as a scientific cultivator of fishes, and knows how to breed and handle perch, bass, salmon, eels, and hornpouts, as well as Illinois farmers do hogs and cattle.

OBJECTS OF THE COMMISSION

The objects of the United States Fish Commission, briefly stated, are: First—To prevent the unnecessary destruction of food-fishes; second—To restore wasted waters to their primitive or more than primitive fruitfulness; and, third—To extend the geographical range of the more important food-fishes, such as shad, salmon and trout, by naturalizing them in new waters. When the New England pilgrims began to fish and build, it seemed incredible that any species of destruction could ever be made to tell upon forests and fisheries, apparently so boundless in extent; but neither our "illimitable" forests or ocean, lake or river fisheries are now regarded as inexhaustible.

Uncle Sam seldom manifests any disposition to look very far into the future; nevertheless, Congress has at length been con-

7. Livingston Stone came to California from New Hampshire in 1872. With the cooperation of the U.S. Fish Commission and the state legislature he established the West's first hatchery, selecting as its site the clear and fast-running McCloud River rather than the larger but more sluggish Sacramento. In the year of Muir's visit, over five million Salmon eggs were produced and shipped to areas as far as New Zealand (they were successfully introduced into that country's rivers). The McCloud hatchery buildings were destroyed by a flood in 1881, and the site now lies under Lake Shasta. For a description of this first California hatchery and a lengthy discussion of the "McCloud" Indians, see Livingston Stone, "Report of the Operations During 1872 at the United States Salmon-Hatchery Establishment on the McCloud River," *U.S. Commission of Fish and Fisheries*, part 2, *Report of the Commissioner* (Washington: Government Printing Office, 1874), pp. 168–215.

vinced that our stores of trees and fishes may be exhausted, and has therefore commenced the manufacture of laws for their protection or restoration. Some fifteen years ago, individual States began to consider the permanent welfare of their fisheries; but it was not until the year 1872 that Congress began to move in the matter. The appropriation for the wants of the Commission for the present year amounts to $30,000.

OBJECT OF THE M'CLOUD RIVER ESTABLISHMENT

The chief object of the establishment at this place is to procure the eggs of the fine large salmon (*salmo quinnat*)[8] for shipment, with a view to the creation of new fisheries and the restoration and improvement of old ones.

WORK ACCOMPLISHED

One million five hundred thousand eggs were shipped from here in the season of 1873, which was the first season of the present establishment.

In the season of 1874, just ended, 5,752,500 were taken, of which 5,100,000 were hatched, and the following quantities shipped. To

Bangor, Me.	100,000
Winchester, Mass.	200,000
Providence, R.I.	100,000
Middletown, Conn.	300,000
Rochester, N.Y.	500,000
Bloomsbury, N.J.	225,000
Marietta, Pa.	300,000
Baltimore, Md.	375,000
Niles, Mich.	750,000
Clarkstown, Mich.	150,000
Boscobel, Wis.	100,000
St. Paul, Minn.	150,000
Ammosa [Anamosa?], Iowa	300,000
Salt Lake City, Utah	150,000

8. *Quinnat* was the pioneer's rendering of the northwest American Indian name for Chinook salmon (*Oncorhynchus tschawytscha*).

Newcastle, Ont., Can.	25,000
New Hope, Bucks Co., Pa.	150,000
Georgetown, Col.	25,000
Randolph, N.Y.	25,000
Rockford, Ill.	50,000
Lynchburg, Va.	50,000
New Zealand	25,000

HOW THE EGGS ARE PROCURED

Toward the end of August the McCloud river salmon are ready to spawn and are then seen pushing their way up toward the sources of the river to deposit it. Mr. Stone has constructed a salmon dam at this place which stretches across the river from bank to bank. In front of this dam the salmon collect in great numbers and keep up a constant plashing in their efforts to leap over it. Most of them are unsuccessful and fall back wearied and glad to rest in the first slow-current eddy. This eddy is a few yards below the dam, and here the tired salmon are captured and the eggs stripped from them into suitable vessels. The eggs are then impregnated by pressing the milt of the male salmon upon them and stirring them gently so as to bring every egg in contact with it. The eggs thus artificially spawned and artificially fecundated are then placed in troughs through which a stream of pure water, carefully filtered, is kept flowing. The eggs measure about 1/3 of an inch in diameter—are pink in color, and look like ripe currants. After they have been in the hatching-troughs about sixteen days the eye-spots of the coming salmonets begin to appear, and they are now ready for shipment. They are packed in boxes, in layers spread upon mosquito-netting, between layers of green, living moss, and these boxes are packed in crates with ice, to keep them cool. In this way, with adequate care and skill in handling, they may be sent safely by ship, wagon, or rail, to great distances. After arriving at their destination they are replaced in hatching-troughs similar to those from whence they were taken, and the hatching progress continued until the young frey break the shell and swim. In procuring the 5,572,500 eggs mentioned above about 5,008 salmon were taken, more than half of which were males.

Thus it will be seen that the berry-like eggs or seeds are stripped from the salmon like peas from a pod. The empty fish-husks average about fifteen pounds, and fall to the share of the Indians, who dry them for winter. It is supposed that all salmon die after yielding their spawn even in the natural way. This destruction, therefore, of so many handsome fish legumes need not be deplored. Here the question is sure to arise, why not capture the breeding salmon and transport them alive to the waters where they are wanted, and allow them to spawn and hatch in their own natural way? Before the discovery of artificial fecundation by Jacobi,[9] this method was the only one known, and is still in practice to some extent. The troutless streams that rush out from cool canyons of the Sierra in the Owens River Valley were stocked last year by a German, who packed trout in cans on the backs of mules from the King's river, Yosemite, over a pass 12,000 feet high.[10] But this more natural method is too slow. Nature does not seem to think of hatching more than one or two in a hundred of the eggs that are spawned, whereas Mr. Stone hatches more than 95 per cent. by the artificial method. In every hundred Nature gives one to the frog, one to the mink, one to the snake, and one to the water-ouzel, etc., and hatches one into a salmon. In like manner the nut-eggs of pine-trees, contained in burrs, are sufficient for the food of many a bird and squirrel as well as for the wants of reproduction.

DESTRUCTION OF FISH—TAMING FISH

Artificial destruction has made lakes and rivers as barren as deserts, so far as fish-food is concerned. Prior to the gold period the Tuolumne abounded in salmon, but the mud of mining de-

9. Hogen Jacobi (1650–1701), Danish naturalist.

10. This is evidently a reference to Joe Boler, a man of "Teutonic pluck and energy," Muir later wrote (see below, "From Fort Independence"), whose ranch lay at the foot of Bloody Canyon near Mono Lake. Nearly all the high country streams and lakes were artificially stocked by Sierra Nevada pioneers. Muir did not foresee how this might upset the high country's ecosystem. The wisdom of this practice went unchallenged for over a century, and the U.S. Forest Service continues to stock certain popular lakes and streams even in designated "wilderness areas," although the Department of the Interior has stopped this artificial intrusion in most national parks.

stroyed them, or drove them away. The Connecticut was also a salmon stream until obstructed by dams, and poisoned by those strangely-complicated filths for which our civilization is peculiar. When fish-ladders are constructed over dams and the sewage of towns and factories is consumed upon the land instead of being poured into the water, leaving paths from the ocean to the spawning grounds free and clean, then our valuable migratory food fishes, such as the shad and salmon, will again become abundant, and that ere long, provided artificial destructions be compensated by artificial reproductions.

Fish may be tamed, and many engage in their culture for the novelty of the thing, or for a natural love of playing and choring in an ichthyological atmosphere, but Stone and his fishy co-workers mean bread and business, and their practical success, considering the infancy of the piscicultural art and the magnitude of the obstacles which had to be overcome, is truly remarkable.

OTHER FISH—HATCHING, ETC.

Besides the harvesting and distribution of McCloud salmon ova, Commissioner Stone brought shad, bass, white fish, eels, horn-pouts and oysters, from the East, mostly for the fructification of California waters. The first aquarium car destined for this State tumbled through the railroad trestle-work into the Elkhorn river, with all its precious fry, much to the discomfiture of Commissioner Stone, who had not the slightest intention of thus casting his shad upon the waters, though some may grow and be found again after many days.

Nearly a million of the eggs taken here this season have been fully hatched and turned into the McCloud river, from whence they were derived, and for this host of wriggling fry the State of California pays the Commission $1,000.

The eggs hatch out into finned fishes in about fifty days, more or less, according to the temperature of the water. When they break the shell they seem eager to try life, and immediately ply their fins. They are then only half an inch long, frail, and semi-transparent, and utterly incapable of gaining an independent livelihood; but nature makes all right by providing each youngling with a bag of provision big enough to last six or seven weeks, and at the end of this period they are grown sufficiently strong to shift for themselves. Their provision sacks are twice as heavy and bulky as their bodies, and they cannot swim far with them at a time. In resting, they frequently lean back, or lie down upon their provision, just as mountaineers do when weary and heavy laden. Long may McCloud salmon swim!

Meantime glaciers and pine-trees rise in vision, and I go to icy Shasta.

McCLOUD RIVER,
OCTOBER 24, 1874

"Edge of the Timber Line on Mount Shasta." Engraver unknown. In Muir, *The Mountains of California*, p. 143.

Muir left the McCloud region to resume his northward journey to
Mount Shasta. The western essayist Joaquin Miller had written of the
Shasta area in several of his short stories, and Clarence King had
published a spirited report of his ascent of the mountain, yet most
Californians knew little about it. Transportation to the region was
limited to coach travel until the following decade, and few pioneers
or tourists knew the area—Muir estimated, for example, that no
more than two dozen visitors came there during the summer of 1874.
That Muir should have been among this group is not surprising,
however, as the grand peak with its glaciers and glacial channels he
believed would teach him something new of wilderness and, he
wrote, of the "mechanical conditions of the fresh snow at so great an
elevation." Muir would stay in the area for more than a month,
making two trips to the summit and once walking around the
mountain's entire base, meanwhile writing the four letters to the
Bulletin which are reproduced below.

Leaving Allen's late in October, traveling alone (Stone was to have
accompanied him but Muir noted to a friend that the commissioner
"had failed of course"[1]), Muir arrived at Shasta and at Justin Sisson's road station shortly afterward, and here he immediately prepared to climb Shasta's summit. Evidently most of the men he met
thought him foolish to make the ascent so late in the season, warning
him of blizzards and snow. ("But I like snow," Muir responded.) He
was aided in preparations for his first climb by Jerome Fay, one of
Sisson's ranchhands. Fay would play a supporting role in a second,
near-fatal climb of the peak. On this first ascent, however, Muir went
alone, and later shared the adventure in the *Bulletin* letter entitled
"Shasta in Winter."

Muir's letter is a carefully balanced report. Not wishing to draw
attention away from his natural subjects of storm and mountain by
underscoring his own courage in withstanding several days and nights
of freezing temperatures, he wanted his readers to understand the
beauty of the severe wildness he had witnessed. Above all he wished
to invest the word *wild* with a new significance for his readers, no
doubt hoping to lead them to the belief that anyone of normal health
could meet and enjoy even the sternest of wilderness adventures.

1. Badè, *Life and Letters,* 2:32.

Thus Muir insists the storm is a "sublime" event, neither to fear nor to avoid. Muir's life may have been in danger during the storm, but his published account takes little notice of any hazard to his personal welfare. Climbing mountains was for him almost a religious act, to be enjoyed and savored, but he rightly suspected his audience would not believe enlightened awareness could result from climbing summits, nor understand his radical view of the true nature and value of mountain experience. The spiritual claims Muir expressed in this article (and in his later letters to the *Bulletin*) he softened through the use of metaphors: the ascent of Shasta takes place against the gentle background of snow drifts that weave a "lavish cross of snow-crystals"; the unearthly scene is pictured as a "land of clouds, undulating hill and dale . . . smooth and rounded as if eroded by glaciers."

He would have his *Bulletin* readers climb the mountains in any weather. The more wild the storm, in fact, the better the lessons offered. When Muir learned the local mountaineers and "wild" teamsters would not venture forth in the snowy conditions, he could not resist concluding his story with the pointed and ironic use of teamster vocabulary. These working men, Muir writes, "dam'd" any storm which flooded their roads. He asks his readers to reach beyond the short-sighted vision of teamsters. Welcome blizzards as well as calms, he insists, for one can hear religion in the earth's storms.

Shasta in Winter

SHASTA STORMS

Snow is falling on icy Shasta.[2] Its rugged glaciers, steep lava-slopes, and broad, swelling base are all gloriously snow-covered, and day and night snow is still falling—snow on snow. The October storms that began a month ago and extended so generally throughout the State, fell with special emphasis upon the lofty cone of Shasta, weaving and felting its lavish cross of snow-crystals, fold over fold, and clothing the whole massive moun-

2. Some of this letter and the previous one Muir used later as he prepared his Shasta chapter of *Picturesque California* (1888). Revised still further, portions appeared in *Steep Trails* (1918), chapters 3 and 4, edited and compiled after Muir's death by William Frederic Badè.

tain in richest winter white. The big dark cluster of November storms was separated from those of October by a week of brilliant sunshine, during which I sauntered leisurely Shastaward, allowing time for the snow, that I knew had fallen, to settle somewhat, with a view to making the ascent of the mountain. This bright lane of cloudless weather was exceedingly buoyant and delightful; every mountain and valley seemed exhilarated with their magnificent storm-bath. The Indian summer disappeared, leaving the atmosphere intensely clear, yet not without a racy autumnal mellowness. The washed colors of the dogwood and the maple shone out gorgeously along every water-course. The pine-needles thrilled and sparkled as if tuned anew; [butter]flies danced in the warm sunbeams; the bent and dripping grasses rose again, and the dainty squirrels came out with every hair of their tails dry and electric, as if they had never known a single rain-drop; even the teamsters, dragging toilsomely through the turn-pike mud, began to swear in lower tones and look hopeful.

A PEDESTRIAN IN THE MOUNTAINS—A ROUGH TRIP

I followed the main Oregon and California stage-road from Redding to Sisson's,[3] and besides trees, squirrels, and beautiful mountain streams, I came upon some interesting men, rugged, weather-beaten fellows, who, in hunting and mining, had been brought face to face with many a Shasta storm. Most of them were a kind of almanac, stored with curious facts and dates and

3. Sisson's Station, earlier known as Strawberry Ranch or Strawberry Valley, was a well-known public stop consisting of a ranch-house, barn, and hotel, advertising itself to be "entertainment for man and beast." This "Shasta Tavern," as it also came to be called, was built by Justin Hinckley Sisson, who had come to California in the 1850s and spent nine years in the mines, returned to Illinois in 1860, married, and once again emigrated to California to construct and operate the hotel in 1864. He acted as postmaster and local guide and was present there at least until 1888, at which time Muir revisited the area to find "Sisson is getting feeble. . . . He deplores the destruction of the forest about Shasta. The Axe and the saw are heard more often in the Shasta woods, and the glory is gone." (Wolfe, *John of the Mountains,* p. 289.) Mount Shasta City now marks the locale of the old Sisson ranch. The local history of the Strawberry Valley region is contained in the memoir "Notes of Mary Southern," n.d., binder no. 6, copy at Castle Crags State Park, California.

ancient weather-notes, extending through a score of stormy
mountain years. Whether the coming winter was to be mild or
severe was the question of questions, and the diligence and
fervor with which it was discussed was truly admirable. A picturesque series of prognostications were offered, based by many
different methods upon the complexion of the sky, the fall of
leaves, the flight of wild geese, etc., each of which seemed
wholly satisfactory only to its author.

A pedestrian upon these mountain-roads is sure to excite curiosity, and many were the interrogations put concerning my little
ramble. When told that I came from town for an airing and a
walk, and that icy Shasta was my mark, I was invariably informed that I had come the wrong time of year. The snow was
too deep, the wind too violent, and the danger of being lost in
blinding drifts too great. And when I hinted that clean snow was
beautiful, and that storms were not so bad as they were called,
they closed the argument by directing attention to their superior
experiences, declaring most emphatically that the ascent of
"Shasta Butte" through the snow was impossible. Nevertheless,
I watched the robins eating wild cherries, and rejoiced in brooding over the miles of lavish snow that I was to meet. Sisson gave
me bread and venison, and before noon of the 2d of November I
was in the frosty azure of the summit.

MOUNT SHASTA—A GLORIOUS PICTURE

In journeying up the valley of the Sacramento one obtains frequent glimpses of Mt. Shasta through the pine-trees from the
tops of hills and ridges, but at Sisson's there is a grand out-
opening both of the mountains and the forests, and Shasta
stands revealed at just the distance to be seen most comprehen-
sively and impressively. It was in the middle of the last day of
October that I first beheld this glorious picture. Gorgeous thickets of the thorn, cherry, birch, and alder flamed around the
meadow. There were plenty of bees and golden-rods, and the
warm air was calm as the bottom of a lake. Standing on the
hotel-veranda, and looking only at outlines, there, first of all, is
a brown meadow with its crooked stream, then a zone of dark
forest—its countless spires of fir and pine rising above one another, higher, higher in luxuriant ranks, and above all the great

white Shasta cone sweeping far into the cloudless blue; meadow, forest and mountain inseparably blended and framed in by the arching sky. I was in the heart of this beauty next day. Sisson, who is a capital mountaineer, fitted me out for calms or storms as only a mountaineer could, with a week's provisions so generous in kind and quantity it could easily be made to last a month in case of a fortunate snow-bound. Of course I knew the weariness of snow-climbing, and the stinging frosts, and the so-called dangers of mountaineering so late in the year, therefore I could not ask any guide to go with me. All I wanted was to have blankets and provisions deposited as far up in the timber as the snow would allow a pack-horse to go. Here I could make a storm-nest and lie warm, and make raids up or around the mountain whenever the weather would allow. On setting out from Sisson's my barometer as well as the sky gave notice of the approach of another storm, the wind sighed in the pines, filmy, half-transparent clouds began to dim the sunshine. It was one of those brooding days that Keith[4] so well knows how to paint, in which every tree of the forest and every mountain seems conscious of the approach of some great blessing, and stands hushed and waiting.

ASCENDING SHASTA IN WINTER

The ordinary and proper way to ascend Shasta is to ride from Sisson's to the upper edge of the timber line,—a distance of some eight or ten miles—the first day, and camp, and rising early push on to the summit, and return the second day.[5] But the

4. William Keith first met Muir in Yosemite in the fall of 1872. The same age as Muir, and sharing Scottish heritage, Keith was to become a famous California landscape artist—with some help from Muir, who here finds an opportunity to say a few good words in behalf of his friend whom he once said was like "a verra brither." Muir's first article to be published in the *Bulletin* was a review of Keith's paintings: see "Art Notes," San Francisco *Daily Evening Bulletin,* June 20, 1874, p. 3.

5. Mount Shasta was evidently scaled as early as 1854. The Whitney Party climbed it in September, 1862. William Brewer then estimated its height to be 14,500'; he also declared there were no glaciers present. See Brewer, *Up and Down California in 1860-1864,* ch. 5. Clarence King, who joined the Whitney Party in 1864, climbed Shasta in 1870 and reported the existence of glaciers the next year in an article published in the *Atlantic Monthly* (September 1871); see also King, *Mountaineering in the Sierra Nevada* (1872), chs. 11-12.

deep snow prevented the horses from reaching the camping-ground, and after stumbling and wallowing in the drifts and lava blocks we were glad to camp as best we could, some eight or ten hundred feet lower. A pitch-pine fire speedily changed the climate and shed a blaze of light on the wild lava slope and the straggling storm-bent pines around us. Melted snow answered for coffee-water and we had plenty of delicious venison to roast.

Toward midnight I rolled myself in my blankets and slept until half-past one, when I arose and ate more venison, tied two days' provisions to my belt, and set out for the summit. After getting above the highest flexilis pines[6] it was fine practice pushing up the magnificent snow-slopes alone in the silence of the night. Half the sky was clouded; in the other half the stars sparkled icily in the thin, frosty air, while everywhere the glorious snow fell away from the summit of the cone in flowing folds more extensive and unbroken than any I had ever yet beheld. When the day dawned the clouds were crawling slowly and massing themselves, but gave no intimation of immediate danger. The snow was dry as meal, and drifted freely, rolling over and over in angular fragments like sand, or rising in the air like dust. The frost was intense, and the wind full of crystal dust, making breathing at times rather difficult. In pushing upwards I frequently sank to my arm-pits between buried lava-blocks, but most of the way only to my knees. When tired of walking I still wallowed forward on all fours. The steepness of the slope—thirty-five degrees in many places—made any species of progress very fatiguing, but the sublime beauty of the snowy expanse and of the landscapes that began to rise around, and the intense purity of the icy azure overhead thrilled every fibre with wild enjoyment and rendered absolute exhaustion impossible. Yet I watched the sky with great caution, for it was easy to see that a storm was approaching. Mount Shasta rises 10,000 feet above the general level in blank exposure to the deep gulf-streams of air, and I have never been in a labyrinth of peaks and canyons where the dangers of a storm seemed so formidable as here. I was, therefore, in constant readiness to retreat into the timber. However, by half past 10 o'clock I reached the utmost summit.

6. The highest trees are white bark pines (*Pinus albicaulis.*)

AMONG THE GLACIERS AND THE LAVA—THE DESCENT

I have seen Montgomery street, and I know that California is in a hurry, therefore I have no intention of saying anything here concerning the building of this grand fire-mountain, nor of the sublime circumference of landscapes of which it is the centre. I spent a couple of hours tracing the outlines of its ancient lava-streams, extending far into the surrounding plains and the pathways of its ancient glaciers, but the wind constantly increased in violence, raising the snow in magnificent drifts, and forming it into long, wavering banners that glowed in the sun. A succession of small storm-clouds struck against the summit pinnacles, like icebergs, darkening the air as they passed, and producing a chill as definite and sudden as if ice-water were dashed in one's face. This is the kind of cloud in which snow-flowers grow, and I was compelled to begin a retreat, which, after spending a few minutes upon the main Shasta glacier and the side of the "Crater Butte," I accomplished more than an hour before dark, so that I had time to hollow a strip of ground for a nest in the lee of a block of red lava, where firewood was abundant.

AMONG THE STORM-CLOUDS

Next morning, breaking suddenly out of profound sleep, my eyes opened upon one of the most sublime scenes I ever beheld. A boundless wilderness of storm-clouds of different age and ripeness were congregated over all the landscape for thousands of square miles, colored gray, and purple, and pearl and glowing white, among which I seemed to be floating, while the cone of Shasta above and the sky was tranquil and full of the sun. It seemed not so much an ocean as a land of clouds, undulating hill and dale, smooth purple plains, and silvery mountains of cumuli, range over range, nobly diversified with peaks and domes, with cool shadows between, and with here and there a wide trunk-cañon, smooth and rounded as if eroded by glaciers. I gazed enchanted, but cold gray masses drifting hither and thither like rack on a wind-swept plain began to shut out the light, and it was evident that they would soon be marshalled for storm. I gathered as much wood as possible, and snugged it shelteringly around my storm-nest. My blankets were arranged, and the topmost fastened down with stakes, and my precious bread-sack tucked in at my head, I was ready when the first flakes fell. All kinds of clouds began to fuse into one, the wind swept past in hissing floods, and the storm closed down on all things, producing a wild exhilaration.

My fire blazed bravely, I had a week's wood, a sack full of bread, and a nest that the wildest wind could not demolish, and I had, moreover, plenty of material for the making of snow-shoes if the depth of the snow should render them necessary.

The storm lasted about a week, and I had plenty to do listening to its tones and watching the gestures of the flexilis pine, and in catching snow-crystals and examining them under a lens and observing the methods of their deposition as summer fountains.

BACK TO SISSON'S

On the third day Sisson sent up two horses for me, and his blankets, notwithstanding I had expressed a wish to be let alone in case it stormed. The horses succeeded in breaking through on the trail they made in coming up. In a few hours more this would have been impossible. The ride down through the forest of silver firs was truly enchanting, the thick flakes falling aslant the noble columns decorated with yellow lichen, and their rich, fronded branches drooped and laden in universal bloom. Farther down, the sugar-pines with sublime gestures were feeding on the storm and waving their giant arms as if in ecstasy. At an elevation of 4,000 feet above the sea the snow became rain, and all the chaparral,[7] cherry, manzanita and ceanothus were bright and dripping.

A GOOD CENTRE FOR STORM NEWS

Sisson's Station seems to be a favorite resort of teamsters as well as of tourists, and one could hardly be more advantageously situated for the reception of storm news. Drivers from Oregon and California meet here almost every night, and while gathered —steaming and mud-bedraggled—around the bar-room fire

7. *Chaparral* is the dense, fire-adapted shrub community commonly found on hot, dry slopes; the name comes from the leather pants once worn by *vaqueros* to protect them from the thorny plants.

compare road and weather notes in terms more picturesque than exact. California storms seem at present to be about as continuous as those of Oregon, for they are alike described as "never letting up," and I can hear of but two species, namely, "dam'd" and "damndest." Meanwhile, the grand storm continues. The wind sings gloriously in the pine-trees. Snow is still falling on icy Shasta, snow on snow, treasuring up food for forests and glaciers and for the thousand springs that gush out around its base.

SISSON'S STATION,
NOVEMBER 24, 1874

The following long letter is Muir's account of the only hunting
expedition he ever joined. Having returned to Sisson's from the
summit storms, Muir encountered a hunting party preparing to travel
into the northeastern section of the region in search of California
bighorn sheep. These animals fascinated Muir, and he seized this
opportunity to study their habits in an area he had not yet visited.
One of the hunters, an Englishman, becomes the hapless recipient of
Muir's pointed barbs in his account of the expedition; another was a
fellow Scotchman whom Muir not surprisingly credits with being the
better woodsman. Sisson and Jerome Fay accompanied the party as
guides. Muir joined but was unarmed.

Muir plays on the word "game" in the title of his letter and in the
opening paragraph, a warning to the reader that what follows may be
an irreverent look at the sport. Indeed, Muir describes the hunt as an
attempt of these restless men-children to kill their boredom. (He
would later write that the Englishman merely sought something with
which to "adorn his halls.") Muir genuinely liked his companions,
and enjoyed his hikes around the strange lava beds of the Modoc
region, but it is evident he was also shocked by the blood-letting of
the experience. The trip seems to have turned his thinking against
hunts. Years later he would even chide President Roosevelt for his
passion for hunting, and suggest that he turn away from such boyish
pursuits.

In Muir's writings of this time and later he suggested that man's
"evolution" (he had read Darwin)[1] might include some progress to a
higher understanding of the rights of animals. Yet, during the hunt,
when he witnessed his companions acting like their "great-grandfathers that were savage as wolves," he admits to having found himself caught up in the wild "blood-letting," feeling "like a wolf
chasing a flying flock,"[2] and concludes that "savageness is natural;
civilization . . . is strained and unnatural." Muir's letter becomes,
then, an attempt to integrate his friends' barbarism with the new
evolutionary theory, by viewing the hunt as a moral lesson. If
hunting has value, it lies in its compression of time, allowing the
hunters a clearer view of what it was they once were. The hunt gives
a telescopic view into their own genetic past. For Muir it becomes a

1. See Engberg and Wesling, eds., *To Yosemite and Beyond*, p. 72.
2. Wolfe, *John of the Mountains*, p. 199.

reminder that only a "few centuries" separate modern man from his caveman ancestors, and it leads him to see how fragile and narrow is the ridge dividing barbarism from civilization. And so what may appear paradoxical—the legendary John Muir participating in the hunting of a rare and endangered species—is in the end resolved as a necessary part of his education in the University of the Wilderness.

In his later narratives of this trip Muir felt it necessary to divorce himself more completely from the hunt. He made it plain he had gone "unarmed" and that the young ewe ("poor woman-sheep") should not have been shot; that upon seeing the remains of a "bonnie yearling" bighorn he thought it had been "a shame to kill it."[3] In an undated note, he later wrote, "Making some bird or beast go lame the rest of his life is a sore thing on one's conscience, at least nothing to boast of, and has no religion in it."[4] It was natural for animals to kill and be killed; it was quite a different thing for evolved man to do the same. These notions Muir arrived at later in life, and only after and because of this trip. With the Shasta game experience over, he would persistently question whether there were not better ways to meet wilderness than to make of it a sport.

Shasta Game

The woods and waters of Shasta contain more wildlife in that form which hunters call *game* than those of any other Alpine region I have ever entered.[5] Trout and salmon in the streams, deer and bears in the forest and wild sheep in the topmost rocks. Winter came early this year, seeming to take even the wild animals by surprise. By the first week of November the storms had

3. Wolfe, *John of the Mountains,* pp. 193-201.

4. Quoted in Edwin Way Teale, ed., *The Wilderness World of John Muir* (Boston: Houghton Mifflin, 1954), p. 314.

5. This letter was reprinted in Wolfe, *John of the Mountains,* pp. 193-200, without the opening paragraph and with Muir's later revisions, some of which are noted below. Parts of the narrative Muir used also in his "Wild Wool," *Overland Monthly* 14 (April 1875). Still another version was combined with portions of "Wild Sheep of California," *Overland Monthly* 12 (April 1874), and appeared in Muir's *The Mountains of California* (1894), ch. 14, "The Wild Sheep."

stripped off most of the bright autumn leaves and bleached all that were left. The robins assembled and fled to warm valleys before their wild cherries were half done. The deer came down into sheltered thickets and stood about as if unable to decide what to do. The bears, too, notwithstanding the warmth of their clothing, began to shuffle out of the snow into the lower canyons and gulches; and when on Mount Shasta I noticed that the wild sheep were also disturbed, as if contemplating removal to their winter pastures. A small flock of about a dozen were sheltering beneath dwarf pines a few hundred yards above my storm-rest.

On my return to the hotel I found four wild hunters—three from Bonnie Scotland, the other from England—all sterling fellows, who, instead of traveling tamely, guide-book in hand, mingle with hunters and trappers, and drink in the grandeur of our matchless wilds in magnificent enfranchisement from all conventions and creeds. Two of this company, Brown and Hepburn,[6] were eagerly bent on hunting the wild sheep, not only for the sport of the thing, but to learn its habits, and see its wild homes, and procure specimens.[7] Sisson, who is himself a keen hunter and an excellent guide to all kinds of game, soon made the necessary arrangements. Blankets, provisions, and rifles were heaped into a wagon, and on the morning of November 8th we set out for Sheep Rock.[8] The party consisted of Sisson as

6. G. Buchanan Hepburn of Scotland was killed "in Mexico or Lower California," according to a note Muir later made.

7. Muir pointedly added in a later version: ". . . and get specimens with which to adorn their halls." Nowhere does he mention the hunters having made any formal study of the Bighorn.

8. Also called Sheep Mountain, elevation 6210'. The hunters were seeking the mountain sheep (*Ovis canadensis californiana*), commonly known as California bighorn. The hunting of bighorn was restricted in California as early as 1872, yet there was no enforcement of the regulations, and so few bighorn survived that by 1883 they were eliminated from the Shasta region. While perhaps one and one-half million bighorn of all species existed in the United States during the early 1800s, fewer than 8,000 survive today, with only an estimated 200 mountain bighorn living in California. See Gale Monson and Lowell Summer, *The Desert Bighorn* (Tucson: University of Arizona Press, 1980). A herd reintroduced to the Shasta region several years ago was inadvertently killed by the National Park Service while it tried to relocate some of the animals; several died in transport and those remaining died of stress.

guide and hunter-in-chief; Jerome [Fay], an enthusiastic hunter in the employ of Sisson, Brown, English, Hepburn, Scotch, and myself. Brown and Hepburn carried double-barreled breech-loading rifles, Jerome and Sisson, Remingtons.

SHEEP ROCK

Sheep Rock lies about 20 miles to the north of here, and is one of the principal winter pastures of the Shasta sheep. It is a mass of lava, presenting a bold, craggy front 2,000 feet high to the gray sage-plains of Shasta Valley. Its summit lies at an elevation of 5,500 feet above the level of the sea, and is several square miles in extent, abounding in grassy hollows where snow never lies deep. Here we hunted only one day. Sheep tracks were no-where abundant. It was, therefore, clear that the brave fellows had not yet been stormed down out of their Shasta pastures. Brown was the only one of the company so fortunate as to catch sight of a single sheep. A massive old ram, with enormous horns, allowed him a special interview, at a distance of twenty steps, but his rifle, unluckily, was not held in place, and the brave Otis, bounding over the lava, played him a handsome farewell.

MOUNT BREMER

Next morning we set out for Mount Bremer, the most noted stronghold of wild sheep in the whole Shasta region, in which large flocks abide both winter and summer. It is distant about thirty miles from Sheep Rock, and five miles from the south shore of the Lower Klamath lake. Our route lay over gray stretches of sage-plain, interrupted by rough lava slopes, timbered with juniper and yellow pine. We camped one night on the edge of a glacier-meadow, arriving early in the afternoon, and after lunch the rifles were carried into the adjacent plains and groves. Hepburn killed a fine buck antelope, which was brought into camp after dark. We had a blazing fire and we brought forward the beautiful stranger into the light and held up his head and steadied him upon his feet. The light fell full upon him, revealing the rare beauty of his color and form and eyes in the most startling manner imaginable. His height at the shoulder was 3 feet; length from nose to root of tail, 5½ feet; length of horns, 7¾ inches; length of tail, 4 inches. Limbs smooth and graceful, somewhat slender, yet expressing abundance of substantial power. Head long, blunt and cow-like; hair, dense and spongy, about two inches long, rich yellowish brown on the back and upper half of the sides, white on the belly and lower half of the sides, with white patch on the buttock, and with three bars of white on the lower half of the neck. The tail white beneath, black above. Along the neck and between the ears the hair is four inches long, and stood erect like a mane. The ears were 7 inches long, stiff and pointed like those of a horse. The eyes, which, though dead, were still beautiful, were situated remarkably high, within one inch of the base of the horns. The antelope (*Antilocapra America*)[9] is still abundant in the dry plains and open pine-woods between Mount Shasta and the Klamath lakes, being seen almost every day in flocks of a hundred or more.

ON BREMER RANCH

On the 11th of November we arrived at the camp and cattle ranch of the Van Bremers,[10] situated near the base of Mount Bremer, and next morning the sheep hunt began in earnest.

9. The animals sought after were the "pronghorn," not a true antelope but an ungulate (*Antilocapra americana*) which is native to North America. Several herds continue to inhabit the lava beds of the northeastern Shasta region. See Ernest P. Walker et al., *Mammals of the World* (Baltimore: Johns Hopkins Press, 1964), 2:141.

10. When pioneers like the Van Bremers moved into the region they displaced the Modoc Indians who, in 1864, were forced to move north to the Klamath Indian Reservation. They returned to the lava bed region and soon were fighting the white settlers for possession of the land. The eldest Van Bremer was among the whites who fought the Modocs. Other Indians of northern California, including the Yahi, Atsugewi, and Achomawi of the Mount Lassen area, were for the most part tolerant of the early settlers until grazing, timbering, and mining intruded too deeply into their territory. The hydraulic mining methods of the 1850s through '70s were especially devastating to the streams and rivers of the area, washing tons of silt and debris into the Sacramento River and its tributaries, flooding the valleys and filling the smaller streams in which the salmon spawned. There is evidence to suggest the Sacramento River was nearly barren of fish as early as 1851, scarcely two years after the arrival of the miners. See "Salmon Fishery on the Sacramento River," *Hutchings' California Magazine* 4:12 (June 1860): 51–56.

The Vans, after whom the mountain was named, are three brothers, who, weary of hunting and trapping, have settled in this splendid wilderness. They assured us we would encounter no other difficulty in finding sheep than wearisome scrambling in rocks and chaparral, and that two hundred or more made their home on the mountain, and reared their lambs there.

Six years ago they all three ascended the mountain with hounds and rifles to make a grand sheep hunt, hoping to capture a score at least, but after pursuing their noble game for a week, their boots and clothes were torn off, and their hounds lamed and worn out, compelling them to abandon the chase after killing only half a dozen, and they have never attempted to hunt wild sheep since. The hounds, though powerful and well-trained, and keeping up the pursuit night and day, failed to run down a single sheep, old or young, so excellent is their endurance and skill. On smooth ground—that is, level or ascending—the hounds would gain upon them, but on descending ground, and on loose, rough, slopes, and jagged lava crags, they fell far and hopelessly behind.

A DAY'S HUNT AND WEARIED HUNTERS—MULE DEER

The morning after our arrival was delightfully crisp and exhilarating; frost crystals covered the sagebrush, and the snows of Shasta glowed rosily in the sunrise. The hunters strode up the bulging slopes of Mount Bremer, full of eager, hopeful life. I spent the day in examining a bluff of fossiliferous sandstone on the shore of Klamath lake, and, on returning to camp at sundown, I found Brown and Hepburn sheepless and weary, declaring that for roughness and general inaccessibility the abodes of Modoc sheep surpassed all the Highland crags and tropic jungles they had ever beheld.[11] It seems that some sixty or eighty head in different flocks were seen during the day, and a few patent bullets from three-hundred-dollar rifles scattered among them without effect.

11. Muir later added he was "glad to hear the sheep had so good a home"; he also made it clear in this revision that he "went unarmed." See Wolf, *John of the Mountains,* pp. 193, 195.

Jerome came in later, reported his having killed a mule deer (*Cervus Macrotis*),[12] which was brought into camp next morning. This proved to be a splendid buck, the first of the species I had seen. His weight, exclusive of the viscera, was 225 pounds; height of the shoulder, 3 feet 7 inches; girth behind the shoulders, 3 feet 10⅞ inches; length from nose to root of tail, 5 feet 7½ inches; length of tail, 6½ inches; length of ears, 10 inches; length of antlers, 2 feet 4 inches. The general color is gray, nearly as in the common black-tailed species; tail white, with a tuft of black hairs 4 inches long on the end; anterior portion of the belly and brisket black; large patch on the buttock white; legs buff.

When the ears were extended horizontally the distance across from tip to tip was 2 feet 1 inch. It is mostly from the size of the ears that this species derives its name, although the whole body is large and mule-like.

The mule-deer is quite abundant here, but it is seldom seen in company with the black-tailed on the western slopes of the Sierra, or on the coast ranges. It is a much larger deer than the black-tailed and less elegant in general form. Its body is not so round, and in every particular, except the antlers, is constructed on a rougher, heavier and stronger plan. Hepburn declared that our specimen was about as grand and shaggy and noble as the red deer of Scotland.

THE HUNT CONTINUED

On the second day of the hunt all the rifles were again carried up the wild mountain, and many sheep were seen, but only one was killed. It was a bonnie yearling lamb, whose horns were only small spikes.[13] After being wounded it still ran nimbly over the lava, followed by our one dog *Guy,* who, according to Jerome, "treed it on a rock," where it was killed by a second shot.

12. The "Black Tail" is one of the four kinds of mule deer in the Sierra, and though it was once thought to have been a separate species (and given the name *Odocoilus columbianus* from its usual habitat), all mule deer belong to *O. hemionus.*

13. Muir was later to add, "It was a shame to kill it." See Wolfe, *John of the Mountains,* p. 196.

Brown and Hepburn were impressed more profoundly than ever with the excellence of Mount Bremer as a sheep castle and with the nobleness of nature's wild sheep, having obtained views of several flocks leaping grandly from rock to rock in full exposure.

So much hard hunting for so little mutton was rather trying, and neither Brown nor Hepburn cared to face the mountain next day. The Vans informed us that large flocks frequently descended the mountain and strolled out into the Modoc lavabeds. We, therefore, determined to hunt in that direction, and as one of the Vans consented to guide us we became sanguine once more. Blankets, etc., were piled into the wagon and driven round to Rett lake,[14] where we were to camp, while the hunters rode in different directions after game; but this day nothing was seen excepting sage-hens and wolves.

SISSON JOINS THE HUNT AMONG THE LAVA CLIFFS

Next day we returned to Van Bremer's, hunting on the way back. Sisson, who had thus far been engaged mostly about camp, set out afoot this morning for a square day's hunting, all by himself, declaring he would "kill a ram before night." Jerome drove round with a wagon, while our guide, Van Bremer, Hepburn, Brown and myself rode straight cross the lava plains between Klamath lake and Mount Bremer, hoping to find game on the way. Nor were we disappointed. We were riding through the sage, in single file, when Van suddenly dismounted and handed me his bridle-rein. I was looking at Mount Bremer at the time, and studying its glacial sculpture, but Van's sharp eyes were looking for sheep, and found them. There they were, fifty or more, rams, ewes and lambs, only sixty or seventy rods off, all in clear sight, on the open plain. The noble animals saw us, however, before we saw them, and stood gazing at us, evidently frightened and feeling caught on account of the levelness of the plain. To the right of them was a jagged battlement of lava; to the left their grand Castle Mountain. They looked ex-

14. Rett Lake (*var.* Rhett Lake) was named by Captain John Fremont in the 1850s; it is now known as Tule Lake Sump. The lava beds Muir describes now form the greater part of Lava Beds National Monument.

"Wild Sheep Jumping over a Precipice." Engraver unknown. In Muir, *The Mountains of California*, p. 319.

citedly this way and that, as if undecided as to which of the two shelters they should flee to. Meanwhile Van and Hepburn ran toward them, crouching in the sage and taking advantage of a slight swell in the ground, while hunter Brown, who was always doing unheard-of-things, had taken his rifle apart and locked it in a box, and sent it home in the wagon like a case of mathematical instruments—a condition of affairs called bad luck. As soon as the hunters' heads began to appear above the swell, the watchful game, seeing the absolute need of moving somewhere, were at length led off toward their mountain by an old ram, all the rest following nearly in single file. The hunters were now within 250 yards, and just as the sheep got under full headway they drew up and took deliberate aim. Van, as he stood with his fourteen-pound rifle to his eye, looked exactly like the figures one sees on powder-flasks; but when Hepburn was aiming, his tall, manly form was slanted back in the sage-brush, like the mast of a clipper ship. Both fired the same moment and down went a noble old ram as if struck with lightning. A moment's silence, and bang went Hepburn's second barrel and down dropped another sheep. Well done Scotch rifle![15] A ram with one barrel, a ewe with the other. The scene was wildly exciting, but gunless Brown sat enveloped in the luck he had manufactured in the morning, speaking not a word; outwardly cool as icy Shasta, but perhaps like that old volcano—hot within. The brave sheep were now bounding wildly over the plain in a direct line for their stronghold, and a bright thought flashed into Brown. He would head the flying game and drive it back to be shot. So, nerving himself as if ready for an English steeple-chase, he dashed his spurless heels upon his calm mustang, but after galloping madly through the sage at the rate of about two miles an hour he was compelled to draw rein in despair. In the meantime, Hepburn's ram rose again, and after staggering a few rods ran firm and erect with its huge horns thrown back over its shoulders. A second shot missed him and he fled like the wind to the shelter of the lava cliffs. This was a fine specimen, apparently full grown, broad-shouldered and massive like a buffalo, and would probably weigh 350 pounds.

15. This line Muir dropped in later versions.

THE SAVAGE ELEMENTS IN MAN—SOME RESULTS

Leading the mean, lean lives we do, we little know how much wildness there is in us. Only a few centuries separate us from great-grandfathers that were savage as wolves; this is the secret of our love for the hunt. Savageness is natural; civilization, at least in this stage of the play, is strained and unnatural. It requires centuries to tame men, while they are capable of being re-savagized in as many years. In the wild exhilaration raised by the running of the game, and the firing, and the pursuit of the wounded, we could have torn and worried like mastiffs, but all this passed away, and we were Christians again. We went up to the ewe, which was "all that was left of them—left of the fifty." She was still breathing, but helpless. Her eye was remarkably mild and gentle, and called out sympathy as if she were human. Poor woman-sheep! She was shot through the head and never knew what hurt her. Bremer drew a big knife and coolly shed her blood, which formed a crimson pool in a hollow of the lava.

It was near sundown and we were five miles from camp. The stars came out, and every trace of excitement faded from our minds. Sisson reached camp just when we did, and reported more blood. He had killed a ram on the mountain and a couple of mule-deer.

Both the ram and the ewe were said by Van Bremer to be considerably below the average size. They measured as follows:[16]

	RAM.		EWE.	
	ft.	*in.*	*ft.*	*in.*
Height at shoulder	3	6	3	0
Girth	3	11	3	3¼
Length from nose to root of tail	5	10¼	4	3½
Length of ears	0	4¾	0	5
Length of tail	0	4¼	0	4½
Length of horns around curve	2	9	0	11½
Distance across, from tip to tip	2	5½	—	—
Circumference of horns at base	1	4	0	6

16. When Muir made measurements of the fallen animals he also carefully inspected their wool with a hand lens. Finding it to be finer than that of domes-

The general color at this season is dull-blue, gray on the sides, and the male nearly black on the legs and belly; the female white on inside of legs and belly, and both with a very conspicuous white patch on the buttocks. The hair is close and spongy, like that of the deer.

LAST DAY OF THE HUNT—A STORM

On the fifth and last day of the hunt the fastnesses of Mount Bremer were invaded once more, but no blood was shed. Brown's luck was, of course, as unique as possible. He had shot elephants in Ceylon, yet no one of these Modoc sheep ever appeared to suspect him of being a hunter, and whether crashing through the brushwood or hammering over the lava blocks with his iron-shod shoes, they still seemed to welcome his approach. To-day he sat down in a lonely place and deliberately took off his shoes, and laid his gun beyond his reach; presently he heard footsteps, and looking round, there stood a ram as if for sacrifice. The grounds of this special familiarity so conspicuous through all the hunt are not easily guessed. Perhaps the secret lay in his color or general brightness. For everything about Brown was bright. His coat was glossy mole-skin, his gun also was unnaturally bright and lay shining on the frosty ground like an icicle, and the nails in his English shoes glittered like crystals of feldspar. There stood the ram, there lay the hunter. He dared not move toward his rifle for fear of breaking up the meeting. Big Horns, therefore, gazed on the brightness undisturbed, and quietly disappeared in the thicket. Brown, however, lay still four hours longer until long shadows grew out over the plain, then returning to camp declared that the shooting of wild sheep was only a matter of time, and that *still* hunting was the only proper method, and after describing the gestures of his visitor and his immense horns, added, with great animation, "I would give twenty English sovereigns to shoot one of these fine fellows."

------

ticated sheep, he said, "Well done for wildness!" Here he found one more argument for the superiority of the natural and wild over its tamed counterpart. This discovery became the theme for his article "Wild Wool," written three months later and reprinted in *Steep Trails* (1918), ch. 1. See also his chapter "The Wild Sheep" in *The Mountains of California* (1894), pp. 300–324.

Some one hinted that an ounce of lead was price enough when properly paid.

The day was all sunshine, and the sun went down in a glow of that delicious purple so common in sagebrush "deserts." But next morning the wind blew stormily and the air was dark with snow-flowers. We intended hunting two days longer to allow time for the arrival of "Brown's luck," but mountain and plain are already white, and a pass of 6,000 feet high lay between us and home, and the danger of being snow-bound so late in the season hastened our departure. Therefore all our game, sheep, deer, antelope, fox, geese and sage-hens were packed and crammed into the wagon and our hunt was done.

SISSON'S STATION,
NOVEMBER 29, 1874

The following short letter is among the rarest of Muir manuscripts. This is due not only to its relative obscurity (it has not appeared in print for over a century) but also and primarily because of the nature of its subject. Muir's lifelong focus was landscape: its appearance and its meaning. In "Modoc Memories," he looks away from this theme to describe instead a historic and tragic human event.

While staying with the pioneer Van Bremers at their ranch near Lake Klamath, Muir joined the eldest Van Bremer's party for a brief visit to the nearby battlefields of the Modoc War. This war had ended only the year before and was still fresh in the mind and conscience of Californians and the nation. The conflict was the last major clash between a Pacific coast Native American tribe and white settlers. The war's origin and course were both tragic and, to some extent, predictable: the Modoc land was overrun by gold-seeking Forty-Niners wishing to avoid the sharper mountain passes of the Sierra Nevada, and in 1853 the Modocs retaliated against the invasion by killing several whites; a few months later some two dozen Modocs were in turn massacred, the killing taking place during a peace parley while both sides were under a flag of truce. Still later, settlers like the Van Bremers arrived to establish homesteads, bringing domesticated sheep herds which competed with the wild bighorn for food and space, and which passed onto the bighorn a disease that eventually exterminated them from the region. By the year 1864, the Modocs, outnumbered and starving, agreed to emigrate north onto the Klamath reservation which they then shared with their traditional enemies. It was an unworkable and degrading experience for the Modocs, and in 1872 several hundred returned to their homeland around Tule Lake to re-establish their life, bolstered perhaps by the Ghost Dance which promised to make them immune to the white man's bullets. They staged a series of raids on nearby ranches, in one instance killing several whites near the Lost River area a few miles north of the region Muir describes in his article.

News of this "massacre" attracted national attention, and outraged whites insisted the Modocs be punished. In the fall of 1872, the U.S. Army arrived with the order to remove the Indians and force them back to the reservation, and the Modoc War was under way. The inevitable killing followed. Captain Jack, the leader of the Modocs, engaged in several brief skirmishes, later succeeding in avoiding entrapment to lead his people into the relative safety of the lava beds. Here they remained for some six months before surrendering in May, 1873. Captain Jack and two other leaders were captured and later hanged. The survivors were sent to Oklahoma.

It was against this background that Muir and his friends arrived in December of the following year. In his letter to the *Bulletin,* Muir recounts some of the major battles of the war, employing a tone strangely uncharacteristic: the region is described as "gloomy" and the former Indian warriors as "devilish." He finds little uplifting in either the land's history or appearance. Muir is repelled both by the war's savageness and by one of his companions' attempt to loot relics. Only in closing does he hint that the landscape might be "redeemed." For the most part, Muir is plainly uncomfortable in this strange land of lava flows and caves, so far removed and so far below the mountains. There is an obvious sense of relief in the final lines of his letter as he takes leave of the tragic place to return once again to the summit and flanks of "white Shasta."

Modoc Memories

VISIT TO THE MODOC LAVA BEDS

"The Lava Beds," rendered famous by the Modoc war, lie on the southern shore of Rhett or Tule lake, at an elevation above sea-level of about 4,500 feet. They are a portion of an ancient flood of dense black lava, dipping north-eastward at a low angle. They are about as destitute of soil as a glacial pavement, and though the surface is generally level, it is dotted with hillocks and rough crater-like pits and traversed in every direction by a net-work of yawning fissures, forming a combination of topographical conditions of a very rare and striking character. While hunting the wild sheep around Mount Bremer,[1] our camp was enlivened with visits from the hunters and trappers, and roving vaqueros of the region. Some of these were as nomadic as Modocs, and had fought in the lava beds, and because the events of the war were still fresh in their minds we were presented with many lively scraps of history and picturesque sketches of the

1. See Muir's previous article, "Shasta Game."

character and personal appearance of Captain Jack, Boston Charley, and Black Jim,[2] most of which had the strangely crevassed and caverned Lava Beds for a background. Our whole party became so eagerly interested that a visit to the war grounds was at once planned, with the eldest Van Bremer, who had fought the Modocs, and was familiar with the whole region, as guide. Our route lay down the Bremer meadows, past many a smooth grassy knoll and jutting cliff, and along the shore of Lower Klamath Lake, thence across a few rough, gray miles of sage plan, making a journey some six or seven hours in length. We got into camp in the middle of the afternoon, on top of a lava bluff 450 feet high.

Toward sunset I sauntered down to the edge of the bluff, which commands a fine map-like view both of the lava beds and the picturesque region adjacent to them. Here you are looking south-eastward, and the grand Modoc landscape, which at once fills and takes possession of you, lies revealed in front. It is composed of three principal parts. There on your left lies a calm lake; on your right a calm forest, and the black lava beds in the middle.

THE LAKE—THE LAVA-PLAIN

The lake is fairly blooming in purple light, and is so responsive to the sky, both in calmness and color, that it seems itself a sky. No mountain shores hide its loveliness. It lies wide open for many a mile, vailed in no other mystery than the mystery of light. The forest also is flooded with sun-purple, and white Shasta rises above it, rejoicing in the ineffable beauty of the alpen glow. But neither the glorified woods on the one hand, nor the lake on the other, can at first hold the eye; it is that dark, mysterious lava-plain between them. Here you trace yawning fissures, there clusters of sombre pits; now you mark where the lava is bent and corrugated into swelling ridges—here again where it breaks in a foam of bowlders.

Tufts of grass grow here and there, and bushes of the hardy sage, but they have a singed appearance and do not hide the

2. Modoc leaders who were convicted of murder and hanged at the conclusion of the Modoc War.

blackness. Deserts are charming, all kinds of bogs, barrens, and heathy moors, but the Modoc lava beds have an uncanny look, that only an eager desire to learn their geology could overcome. The sun-purple slowly deepened over all the landscape, then darkness fell like a death, and I crept back to the blaze of the camp-fire.

A TRAGIC SPOT—THE MODOC STRONGHOLD

Next morning the Modoc plains and mountains were born again, and Van Bremer led us down the bluff. Just at the foot you come to a square, inclosed by a rough stone wall. It is a graveyard, where some thirty soldiers lie, most of whom met their fate on the 26th of April, surprised by the Modocs while eating lunch, scattered in the lava beds, and shot down like bewildered sheep.[3] Picking our way over the strange ridges and hollows of the "beds," we come, in a few minutes, to a circular flat a score of yards or so in diameter, where the comparative smoothness of the lava and a few handfuls of soil have caused the grass tufts to grow taller. This is where General Canby met his fate.[4] From here our guide led us around the shore of the lake to the main Modoc stronghold, a distance of about two and a half miles. The true strongholds of Indians are chiefly fields of tall grass, brushy woods, and shadowy swamps, where they can crouch like panthers and make themselves invisible, but the Modoc castle is in the rock. When the Yosemite Indians made raids upon the early settlers of the lower Merced they withdrew with their spoils into Yosemite valley, and the Modocs are said to have boasted that in case of war they possessed a stone house into which no white man could come. Notwithstanding the height and sheerness of Yosemite walls, the Indians were unable to hold it against the soldiers for a single day, but the Modoc castle was held defiantly for months. It consists of numerous re-

3. Captain Evan Thomas led about seventy soldiers into the Schonchin Flow region of the lava beds in pursuit of the Modoc warriors and their families; approximately two-thirds of his men were killed in the Modoc victory.

4. Captain Jack was persuaded by some of his followers to assassinate General E. R. Canby during a peace discussion and while under a flag of truce. The site of this incident is marked by "Canby's Cross" in Lava Beds National Monument.

"The Modocs in Their Stronghold." Cover, *Harper's Weekly* 17:853 (May 3, 1873).

doubts, formed by the unequal subsidence of portions of the lava flow, and of a complicated network of redans abundantly supplied with salient and re-entering angles, and these redans are united with one another and with the redoubts by a labyrinth of open and covered corridors, some of which expand at intervals into spacious caves, forming altogether the strongest and most complete natural Gibraltar I ever beheld.

Other lava castles, scarcely less strong, are connected with this by subterranean passages known only to the Indians, while the unnatural blackness of the rock out of which nature has constructed these defenses and the weird inhuman physiognomy of the whole region are well calculated to inspire terror of themselves. Before coming to the battle-ground we frequently heard it remarked that our soldiers merited the fate that befell them. "They were unplucky," "too uncautious," "too drunk," etc. But here we could only pity the poor fellows called to so deadly a task.

THE MODOC CAPTURE

In the capture of this Modoc castle there was no scope for what is known as "brilliancy and knightliness." The strategy of a Von Moltke, or impetuous valor of a Hotspur were alike inapplicable, nor was it possible to achieve here any of that class of bulky victories styled "glorious" which fill newspapers and are followed in due course of time by clerical hallelujahs. On the contrary it was all cat-crouching and gliding—every soldier for himself—while the flinty jaggedness of the ground was such that individual soldiers could scarce keep themselves together as units; one limb straddled here, another there; and while thus sprawling to the assault, unseen rifles were leveled upon them with deadly aim. On the other hand, the Modocs were at home. They had hunted the wild sheep and the bear in these lava beds; now they were hunting men in the very same way. Their guns were thrust through chinks while they lay safely concealed. If they wished to peer above their breast-works they tied bunches of sage-brush around their heads. They were familiar with byways both over and under ground, and could at any time sink out of sight like squirrels among bowlders. Our bewildered soldiers heard and felt them shooting, now before them, now behind them, as they glided from place to place along fissures and subterranean passes, all the while maintaining a more perfect invisibility than that of modern ghosts. Modocs, like most other Indians, are about as unknightly as possible. The quantity of the moral sentiment developed in them seems infinitely small, and though in battle they appear incapable of feeling any distinction between men and beasts, even their savageness lacks fullness and cordiality. The few that have come under my own observation had something repellant in their aspects, even when their features were in sunshine and settled in the calm of peace; when, therefore, they were crawling stealthily in these gloomy caves, in and out on all fours, unkempt and begrimed, and with the glare of war in their eyes, they must have looked very devilish. Our guide led us through the mazes of the castle, pointing out its complicated lines of redoubts and redans, and our astonishment at the wild strength of the place was augmented at every turn.

CAPTAIN JACK'S CAVE—GEOLOGICAL PHENOMENA

Captain Jack's cave is one of the many sombre mansions of the castle. It measures about 25 or 30 feet in diameter at the opening, and extends but a short distance in a horizontal direction. The floor is littered with bones and horns of the animals slaughtered for food during the war—a good specimen of a human home of the Stone Age. The sun shines freely into its mouth, and graceful bunches of grasses and eriognae and sage grow around it, redeeming it from all its degrading associations, and making it lovable notwithstanding its unfinished roughness and blackness. One of our party was a relic-seeker and we were unremitting in our endeavors to satisfy his cravings. Captain Jack's drinking-cup, fragments of his clothing, buttons, etc., were freely offered, but only gold watches or pistols said to have been plundered from the dead and hidden in some of these endless caves were sufficiently curious for his refined tastes.

The lava beds are replete with phenomena of great geological interest. Here are true fissures from a few inches to 8 or 10 feet in width, abrupt and sheer-walled as the crevasses of glaciers, and extending continuously for miles. Miniature hills and dales also and lake basins and mountain ranges, whose formation is due neither to direct upheaval nor to erosion. Where the lava meets the lake there are some fine curving bays beautifully embroidered with rushes and polygonums, a favorite resort of waterfowl.[5] Riding homeward we created a noisy plashing and beating of wings among the cranes and geese, but the ducks were

5. The region Muir describes is now designated Tule Lake National Wildlife Refuge. The flower is the American bistort (*Polygonum bistortoides*), once an important food source for the Modocs.

more trustful and kept their places, merely swimming in and out through openings in the rushes, and rippling the glassy water on which the sun was beaming. The countenance of the lava beds became beautiful. Tufts of pale grasses, relieved on the jet-rocks, looked like bouquets on a mantel; besides, gray and orange lichens, cushions of green mosses appeared, and one tuft of tiny rock-fern. Bountiful Nature gives all this "beauty for ashes" in this sombre region of volcanic fire.

"When California was wild," John Muir was to write in his first
book *The Mountains of California* (1894), "it was one sweet bee-
garden throughout its entire length, north and south, and all the way
across from the snowy Sierra to the ocean." Muir's interest in the
bee dates at least from this first trip to Shasta, and later he was often
to hold up the bee as the "sweetest" symbol of free and joyous
wildness.

Muir was glad to be rid of the dark memories of the Modoc
region, and the study of the little bees was a welcome counterpoint.
In the following letter he uses the bee and a bee "point-of-view" as a
natural vehicle for giving the glacial history of Shasta. He then invites
his readers to "quit their cities" and "come a beeing." Forget hunting even, he tells them, "let blood alone," and enjoy the pure wildness of the honey bees which have been "let alone to follow their
own sweet ways." Clearly by the time Muir composed this letter he
had adopted his new role as spokesman for the mountains, declaring
at one point in the letter his wish to "clear my skirts from the
responsibility of silence by shouting a cordial *come*. Come a beeing;
huckleberry bogs in full bloom are glorious sights. . . . take a
baptism and a honey-bath and get some sweetness into your lives."
After the sombre experience of the lava beds he was again home.
"Shasta Bees" is among the finest and most timeless invitations to
wilderness to be found among his *Bulletin* contributions. Everything
he wrote after leaving Yosemite either instructed or courted his
readers, but nowhere does Muir better describe the gentle wilderness
than in this letter.

Shasta Bees

The Shasta woods are full of wild bees, and their honey is
exactly delicious.[1] At least such was the quality of my samples,

1. Muir knew San Francisco readers would be interested in bees. The sale and
export of honey was fast becoming a key economic factor in the state, and thousands of Californians were setting up their own backyard apiaries with the dream
of quick wealth. Some 20,000 hives existed in Los Angeles by 1878, and an addi-

and no wonder, inasmuch as it was in great part derived from the nectar bells of a huckleberry bog by bees that were let alone to follow their own sweet ways. The hive was a living pine-tree, and the distance to the honey-bells was only a moment's buzz. Bees themselves could hardly hold the conception of a more honeyful place—honey-bog to left of them; honey-bog to right of them; blooming willows for springtime; golden-rods for autumn; and beside a'that and a'that, miles of acres of butter-cups and columbines and rosy chaparral. Regarding Mount Shasta from a bee point of view and beginning at the summit, the first 5,000 feet is clothed in summer with glaciers and rags of snow, and is, of course, almost entirely honeyless. The next 1,000 feet of elevation is a brown zone tufted and matted with bush penstemon and bryanthus.[2] Next comes the silver-fir zone, about 2,500 feet in height, containing few sweet flowers, but rich in honey-dew and pollen. Next the zone of honey-bearing chap-arral or Shasta heather, forming the smooth, sunny slopes of the base. This last is six or seven miles wide and has a circumference of more than seventy miles. Companies of spruce and pine break across it in well-watered sections; yet, upon the whole, it is remarkably regular and contains all the principal honey-grounds of the mountain.

THE BEE LANDS

The formation of the Shasta bee lands is easily understood. Shasta is a fire-mountain, created by a succession of eruptions of ashes and molten lava, which, pouring over the lips of the craters, layer over layer, grew outward and upward like the

---

tional 24,000 were to be found in San Diego, whose honey export in one year was over 90 tons during the summer months. When Muir prepared *The Mountains of California* (1894), he used portions of "Shasta Bees" for a chapter entitled "The Bee-Pastures." Here he noted that a "man unsuccessful in everything else" will content himself to "buy a few colonies . . . take them back to the foot of some canyon where the pasturage is fresh, squat on the land, with or without the per-mission of the owner, set up his hives, make a box cabin for himself, scarcely bigger than a beehive, and await his fortune."

2. *Bush penstemon:* possibly mountain pride. *Bryanthus:* Muir probably meant *Phyllodoce breweri,* red heather.

trunk of an exogenous tree. During the glacial period³ the whole Shasta cone was capped with ice, which by erosion degraded it to some extent and remodeled its flanks. When at length the glacial period began to draw near a close the ice-cap was gradually melted off around the bottom, and in receding and breaking up into its present condition deposited those irregular heaps and rings of moraine matter upon which the Shasta forests are growing. The glacial erosion of most of the Shasta lavas gives rise to soils composed of rough bowlders of moderate size and a great deal of light, porous, sandy *detritus,* which yields very readily to the transporting power of running water. An immense quantity of this finer material was sorted out and washed down from the upper slopes of the mountain by an ancient flood of extraordinary magnitude, and redeposited in smooth, delta-like beds around the base. These form the main honey-grounds. The peculiar vegetation for which they were planned was gradually acquired, huckleberry bogs were planted, the seasons became summer, the chaparral became sweeter, until honey distills like dew. In this glorious honey zone the Shasta bees rove and revel, clambering in bramble and huckle-bloom, ringing and singing, now down among buttercups, now out of sight in the rosy blossoms of the buckthorn. They consider the lilies, and roll into them; and like lilies they toil not, for bees are run by sun-power, just as mill-wheels are by water-power, and when the one has plenty of water and the other plenty of sun they hum and quiver alike.

I have often thought in bright, settled sun weather, that I could tell the time of day by the comparative energy of bee movements. Gentle and moderate in the cool of the morning,

3. Muir believed the Sierra, and here the southern portion of the Cascades, was once under the ice of a single Glacial Epoch. Later geologists found that there were at least four distinct ice periods on this continent. The glaciers which Muir found in Yosemite, beginning in 1871 with the Black Mountain glacier, and the glaciers Clarence King discovered on Shasta and which Muir is here describing, are not residual ones from the Great Ice Age but rather are independent masses which have been growing and retreating for a period of several hundred years. Muir is entirely correct, however, in his description of moraine formation and glacial erosion on and around Shasta.

gradually increasing in fervor, and at high noon thrilling and quivering in wild sun-ecstasy.

Bees are as directly the outcome of bright light as flowers are. Bee death and flower death are also alike—merely a sun-withering and evaporation.

Shasta bees appear to be better fed than any other I know of. They are dainty feeders and enormously cordial withal. Mint moths and humming-birds seldom set foot on a flower, but reach out and suck through long tubes as through straws; but bees hug and clasp and rub their blunt countenances upon them like round, awkward children upon their mothers.

DELIGHTFUL REGION

Of all the overworked and defrauded toilers of California towns, only about twenty came to the daylight of Shasta last season. How the glories of this region have been so long unvoiced when the Oregon and California stage has run daily past for years on the very skirts of the great white cone, is a mystery. There is no daylight in towns, and the weary public ought to know that there is light here, and I for one clear my skirts from the responsibility of silence by shouting a cordial *come.* Come a beeing; huckleberry bogs in full bloom are glorious sights, and they bloom twice a year. The flowers are narrow-mouthed purple bells that seem to have caught the tones of the alpen glow. Later, these blooms turn to berries, and the leaves to crimson petals. Here you may go with the bees. Conceive if you can the magnetism of brushing through the bushes with myriads of honey-bees singing against your knees, and, besides, no softness ever enjoyed by human foot is comparable with the softness of a bog. Come all who need rest and light, bending and breaking with over work, leave your profits and losses and metallic dividends and come a beeing. It is hard to die the dark death of towns, hearse, coffin, cloth and countenances all black. In June the base of Mount Shasta will be as white with honey bloom as the summit with snow. Follow the bees and be showered with blossoms; take a baptism and a honey-bath and get some sweetness into your lives.

If you like to think, there is plenty here to think at. How Shasta fires have burned and builded, and how, notwithstanding it is still hot within, glaciers dwell on its flanks; and how as one of the grand ashy hearths of nature its base flows with honey. Geology, botany, zoology, grand object lessons in each, and if you like hunting there is game in abundance. But better let blood alone and come purely a beeing. The honey grounds will be blooming in June.

Sisson's Station,
December 17, 1874

PART TWO
Home in Yosemite

Going to the mountains is going
home, and gladly we climbed higher,
higher, through the freshened piney
woods—over meadows, over streamlets, over waving ridge and dome.

July 1875

The winter storms of 1874–75 drove Muir down from Shasta's slopes
and back to the "town dark" of Oakland and San Francisco and to
"that Yosemite book" yet to be completed. Friends—most especially
Mrs. Carr—were urging him to settle down long enough to produce
the volume; he knew the book's major outline, and evidently finished
the manuscript sometime during the winter. Upon its completion,
Muir wrote to his sister that it had been sent to an eastern publisher,
but presumably the papers were not published, and the manuscript is
now lost.

But before returning to cities and manuscripts, Muir visited the
Feather and Yuba river region of California. Living in the small town
of Knoxville (on some maps called Brownsville) was Muir's friend
Emily Pelton, whom he had met a decade before during a stay in
Prairie du Chien, Wisconsin. Muir wished to see this lady friend he
had almost certainly once considered marrying, and to spend the last
precious moments of the season exploring the region's foothills and
tracing its geology. It was during this visit to the Knox family that he
climbed a tall fir during a windstorm—a treat he later described in his
article "A Windstorm in the Forests of the Yuba" (*Scribner's
Monthly,* November, 1878; revised and reprinted in *The Mountains
of California*). Muir also witnessed the Yuba River in full flood, an
awesome display of nature's power which, like the glacial carving of
valleys, he was later to describe as a paradoxical model of creation
through destruction. By his persistent iteration of this theme (for
example, in several *Bulletin* writings of the following summer), Muir

"Yo-Semite Valley, Mariposa Co. Cal." Lithograph by the Nahl Brothers, San Francisco, after a drawing by T. A. Ayers. Originally published by Hutchings and Rosenfield, 1859; reproduced in Hutchings, *Scenes of Wonder and Curiosity in California*, p. 144. Courtesy the Bancroft Library.

made it clear that he wanted his readers to revolutionize their values and their sense of cause and effect. He hoped the flood would be warmly received by readers, notwithstanding his acknowledgment that it would be remembered more for "drifted bridges and houses that chanced to lie in its way than for its own beauty, or for the thousand blessings it brought to the fields and gardens of nature."[1]

Muir spent the winter in San Francisco at the home of John Swett. In April he again climbed Mount Shasta (this time as a guide for the Coast and Geodetic Survey) and two days later made a second ascent in the company of Jerome Fay. The pair were caught in a tremendous snowstorm while near the summit and survived only because they found some warmth by sleeping near the mountain's sulphurous hot spring. Muir said he "nearly lost all" as the "intense cold and want of food and sleep made the fire of life smoulder and burn low." Still he counted it among his life's richest moments, and he would tell and retell the story of that stormy night for years to come.[2]

Muir resumed his *Bulletin* articles the following June, and here we pick up his story and his writing. He returned to his cherished Yosemite to study the region's forests and begin a survey of the Sierra's Big Tree groves, which more and more were becoming his chief interest. This shift from geology to botany would greatly affect his philosophy of conservation, and it noticeably altered the intent of his articles. As the forests became his focus, so did an increased awareness of the dangers threatening their existence.

Bulletin editors were evidently convinced other articles would follow Muir's first letter about tourism and forests, and headlined this article and those which followed "Summering in the Sierra." Muir was to write eleven articles for the *Bulletin* during the summer, ten of which are reproduced below. (One, entitled "The Southern Limit of the Sequoia," was presumably written but not published.) Taken together, they reveal Muir's conversion from student of the wilderness to its professor and protector. One can trace an almost weekly development of concern. These letters find him describing the dangers threatening the state's forests: sheepmen and lumber companies and monopolists in nearly every ridge and valley of the Sierra. When the season was over and his traveling done, Muir would appeal

1. "Flood-Storm in the Sierra," *Overland Monthly* 14 (June 1875).
2. See especially Muir's "Snow-Storm on Mount Shasta," *Harper's Magazine* 55 (September 1877): 521-30; and "A Perilous Night on Shasta's Summit," *Steep Trails* (1918), ch. 3.

to the state government to protect the trees and the watershed regions
of California.

During the early summer of 1875 it was still the Yosemite forests
which most awakened his imagination and brought out his best
writing. Many of Muir's themes come together in the following three
articles: tourists and geology, trees and friends (and trees as friends),
animals and plants.

Muir's opening *Bulletin* article, subtitled "The Summer Flood of
Tourists," summarizes his glacial theories and describes the infant
tourist industry of Yosemite Valley as "one of the most hopeful and
significant signs of the times." He then draws a playful parody of
himself as Yosemite Guide, suggesting to his readers that the best way
to "do the Valley" is to sit motionless beneath a willow, idly watching nature's deliberate show. Clearly, in returning to Yosemite, Muir
had gone home.

The Summer Flood of Tourists

As soon as the winter snow melts, an ungovernable avalanche
of tourists comes pouring pell mell into Yosemite, flooding the
hotels, and chafing and grinding against one another like rough-
angled bowlders in a pothole. The cause of this disorder, so de-
structive to all real enjoyment, is the strange misconception that
Yosemite is the only feature of the Sierra worth seeing; that the
falls form the main feature of Yosemite; and that the falls,
unless seen in the nick of time, that is during the spring flood,
are not worth seeing at all. Now, I would by no means seek to
divert travel from Yosemite to other valleys of the range, because few travelers have the necessary time and money for more
extended excursions, and perhaps no other valley offers as great
a quantity of all that is most beautiful and sublime in mountain
scenery. Yet, nevertheless, one's enjoyment of a visit to Yosemite will be heightened and made more rational, and be divested
of much of its feverish friction by a recognition of the simple
fact that the variable waterfalls form only a subordinate feature
of the valley, while its sublime architecture, and the lofty moun-

tains by which it is surrounded remain almost unchanged and unchangeable throughout the year.

YOSEMITE FALLS—YOSEMITE CREEK

As far as the falls are concerned, it seems to be pretty generally believed that the greater the quantity of water the greater the beauty; and it certainly seems pathetic that at this stage of human evolution it should be necessary to state that every waterfall has an individual character, and that each possesses a series of beauties changing with the seasons, all the varying types of beauty blending with one another inseparable and incomparable.

The broad rocky basin from which the waters of Yosemite Fall are derived has a more southerly exposure than any other Yosemite basin; therefore, its stream is the first in flood and the first to fail in summer heat. Only one of its larger affluents takes its rise in perpetual snow, while Nevada creek,[3] that forms the Nevada and Vernal Falls, sends back many a branch to the eternal snow and ice of the very summit of the range. Consequently, it is the last to become flooded, and the last to reach low-water mark.

Yosemite creek is usually at its greater height between the months of May and June and at its lowest between October and November. The first winter storm usually falls on the mountains some time in December, after which it flows with a moderate current all winter. When the stream is lowest it is a mere dribble. During the spring freshet it is about thirty feet wide and ten feet deep, with a current running eight or ten miles an hour, measured just at the top of the wall before it makes the tremendous leap. The average summer size, measured at the same place, is about twenty feet wide and three feet deep, with a current of three or four miles an hour. The winter size is somewhat less. The Nevada Bridal Vail and Illionette[4] reach their highest devel-

3. *Nevada creek:* Merced River. This is the only instance in which Muir used the term. Perhaps he thought the name Merced River should be applied only beyond the point where the Tenaya Creek joins the main current.

4. Bridalveil and Illiouette Falls.

opment a week or two later, and flow with fine, stately, well-sustained currents all through the summer.

THE SEASONS IN THE GREAT VALLEY

Spring tourists will find flooded meadows and waterfalls, with few flowers. Those of summer will find a maximum of birds and flowers, and water of finer forms and voices, but less emphatically sublime. In autumn the loud booming thunder tones of the falls are hushed, and all their waters are woven into lace. Glorious clouds of color are displayed along the river-bank in thickets of maple and dogwood and poplar; and all around the meadows, in patches of withered brecken and straggling groves of oak—every color enhanced by floods of thick golden sunshine, and by the delightful calmness and repose of Indian summer ripeness. In winter the rocks and trees wear the divine jewelry of snow and ice; booming avalanches shoot from heights like waterfalls, and mountain storms are beheld in all their imposing grandeur. Thus all times and seasons are best for visiting Yosemite Valley. Nature is still living and working. Her hand still rests on rock and water and sky, fashioning her glorious temple to more completeness and beauty. The varying changes that circle round the year are thus seen to be notes of one harmony, and the man who comes with ears to hear will hear.

YOSEMITE TOURISTS

The Yosemite stream of tourist travel is one of the most remarkable on the globe, taking its rise in every nation, and forming one of the most hopeful and significant signs of the times. Here, however, we have no intention of sinking out of sight in the philosophy of the thing, yet we may be indulged in remarking, that like all the rivers of California, these streams of sight-seeing travel are all post-glacial in age, and that they flow up mountains instead of down. The western or Japan tributary of the Yosemite travel stream is more masculine and indefectible than the eastern, yet all Yosemite tributaries seem to suffer mysterious perturbations in the vicinity of San Francisco. Road-agents, hired runners and other similar forces may perhaps be the chief causes of the phenomena. Tourists should avoid agents as much as possible. There is not the slightest difficulty in getting into the valley, choose which way you will.

ROADS TO THE VALLEY

Three well-constructed wagon roads conduct into the valley, viz., the Mariposa, Coulterville and Big Oak Flat, and according to the rival measurements of the several agents all three are the shortest, least dusty, and conduct through the finest scenery. It seems to me there is no great choice between the several routes; all are good, for it is impossible to reach Yosemite without passing through the grandest forest scenery in the world. As far as miles are concerned, the Mariposa route is perhaps the longest, the Big Oak Flat the shortest, but all necessarily pass through the same forest groves; and to those who love leafy dells, cool rushing streams, and flowing wooded ridges plaited together in graceful braids, the longest route will be the best.

"DOING" THE VALLEY

Once arrived in the valley and choice made of the hotels, it is important to know what to do with one's self. I would advise sitting from morning till night under some willow bush on the river bank where there is a wide view. This will be "doing the valley" far more effectively than riding along trails in constant motion from point to point. The entire valley is made up of "points of interest." Sunlight streaming over the walls and falling upon the river and silvery foliage of the groves; the varied rush and boom of the falls; the slipping of the crystal river; birds, flowers, and blue, Alpine sky, are then seen most fully and impressively, without the blurring distractions of guiding, riding and scrambling. Few, however, will believe this, and anxious inquiries will always be made for ponies, points, and guides. Perhaps the best of the special points is Glacier Point, reached from the valley by a fine, wide trail, from which all the main rocks and falls are seen in striking positions and combinations.[5] After a height of about 500 feet is reached, a wide sweeping view is obtained down

5. Muir claimed to have coined the term "Glacier Point" in the early 1870s, at the very time his lengthy debate with Josiah Whitney concerning the creation of the Valley was in its heated beginnings. Muir's claim seems valid since it was he

the valley over the tops of the thickest pines between the Cathedral Rocks and El Capitan. Higher, the Merced is seen curving tranquilly through meadow and grove, the crystal river complementing the white booming falls, and the green, richly-broidered meadows, the massive granite rocks. At an elevation of 1,500 feet the upper portion of the valley comes into view, bounded by the great Half Dome, poised majestically in the pure azure like the very Goddess of the Valley.

VIEW FROM GLACIER POINT

From Glacier Point we look down over the edge of a sheer granite wall 3,000 feet upon soft green meadows and innumerable spires of yellow pine. On the opposite side of the valley the sculpture of the walls is seen in grand proportions; the Royal Arches, North Dome, Indian Canyon, Eagle Cliff, and beyond the dome-paved basin of Yosemite creek, Mt. Hoffmann, Cloud's Rest, Mt. Starr King girdled with forests, the glacier-carved peak of the Merced group. The dark, crowded clusters of the Lyell group, wide swaths of forests growing upon ancient moraines, all of which are in clear view, forming one of the noblest Alpine landscapes the eye of man ever beheld; while the Vernal, Nevada and Yosemite Falls sing in full accord, plainly heard as if we were standing in their spray. Here the attentive observer will not fail to perceive that all this glorious landscape is new-made, newly brought to light from beneath the universal ice sheet of the glacial period, and that the loftiest domes were overswept by it just as bowlders are overswept by a flood of water. Hence, all the hardest and most resisting portions of the landscape are also the highest. Every dome, ridge and mountain in the fore and middle has rounded outlines, while all those of the summit peaks are spiky and sharp, because the former were *over*-flowed by the heavy, grinding folds of the ice sheet, while the latter were *down*-flowed, thus grinding them into sharp, jagged blades.

Here you see the tributary valleys of the main Yosemite Trunk Valley branching far and wide back into the fountains of perpetual ice and snow on the axis of the range. Adown these wide pol-

---

who first insisted on the glacial origin of Yosemite Valley. The pathway here referred to is the "Four Mile Trail," originally a toll trail completed in 1872.

ished valleys once poured the ancient glaciers that united here to form the main trunk glacier that eroded the valley out of the solid granite, wearing it gradually deeper, chip by chip, block by block, particle by particle, moving on throughout the countless seasons of the ice age, unhalting, unresting, until every rock was fashioned and sculptured to the glorious beauty they now possess.

SNOW-CLAD PEAKS—TRAVEL

Mounts Hoffman, Lyell, Ritter, and all their lofty companion peaks lying to the east of the valley, are still laden with snow, and the streams derived from them are flowing with fine confident currents, although the time of Spring freshets is already past. This year travel began to slip and rush to the valley some two weeks earlier than usual on account of the lightness of last winter's snows; but the dolorious outcry raised concerning crowded hotels was caused by the closing of the Hutchings Hotel,[6] and not by any great increase of travel over other years. All the hotels are now open and in order, with ample accommodation for everybody. Therefore let all come who will.

PERSONAL—SNOW-FALL

Keith's health is improving in response to the delicious pine scented air, and he is absorbing mountain beauty as the pines absorb the light. Our party, composed of Swett, Keith, and McChesney[7] will set out for the High Sierra to-morrow. Six inches of snow fell yesterday around Yosemite walls, but the clouds are breaking, sunshine is pouring over the wet domes, and every leaf and flower is shining.

YOSEMITE VALLEY,
JUNE 14, 1875

6. James Hutchings had visited the Valley in the 1850s, settled for awhile in San Francisco where he edited *California Magazine,* then returned to Yosemite in 1859 to claim 160 acres and operate a hotel. Muir was given a job by Hutchings, but the two men were not close friends. It may be that a jealous Hutchings thought his young wife showed too much interest in Muir. Muir left Hutchings's employment declaring "he was not kind to me." Hutchings gave up his private claim in 1874 and was compensated with $24,000 by the California legislature.

7. John Swett and J. B. McChesney, friends of Jeanne Carr; and William Keith, the landscape artist.

Muir's next two letters describe a trip from Yosemite's Crane Flat to
Tuolumne Meadows and over the crest of the Sierra to Mono Lake.
He is joined on this trek by his friend John Swett, an Oakland
acquaintance named J. B. McChesney, and the artist William Keith.
It is in this letter that Muir most strongly tests his readers' con-
ventional reasoning by stating, "all that we call destruction is creating
. . . it is just where storms fall most violently that the greatest
quantity of beauteous, joyous life appear." Muir plainly enjoys this
return to the region where he had spent his first summer in the
Sierra.

The following Yosemite letters are among his best public statements
in praise of the wilderness experience. The first short letter, entitled
"A Winter Storm in June," culminates in one of his finest descriptions of the subalpine forests: "The purple cones are sprinkled over
the bluish green foliage from top to bottom, and the whole tree is a
poem, not a single prose leaf, or branch, or motion, is ever visible."

A Winter Storm in June

GENTRY'S STATION, NEAR YOSEMITE, JUNE 17TH

June storms are not altogether rare in the Sierra, yet they are
seldom so extensive as the one just completed. A foot or more of
snow and hail fell on the mountains adjacent to Yosemite on the
15th and 16th ultimo, covering flowers and ferns, and loading
down the branches of the Pine trees. On the morning of the
15th, Half Dome was encircled with clouds, and the Upper Fall
was torn into shreds and streamers by gusty storm winds like
those of winter, and every pine and cedar waved their green
plumes in lively expectation of a storm. Our party[1] were unwilling to wait fair weather, and at once began to climb out of
the valley in long cavalcade with the inevitable mules, mustangs
and camp *debris*. Before we had fairly passed the brow of El

1. Muir was accompanied by John Swett, William Keith, and J. B. McChesney, whom Muir later refers to as "Mack."

Capitan rain began to fall, and dark swift-moving clouds descended on many a beetling cliff and rock-front, finally forming a dense continuous ceiling from wall to wall. On reaching Gentry's Station—1,800 feet above the Valley—the storm began to abate, and we deliberated whether to push on to the Eagle Meadows, lying to the north of the Valley, or to camp where we were. Mack and Swett seemed inclined to go on, when Keith suddenly broke up the council by declaring, with a scowl darker than a storm-cloud, that it was "perfect madness for poets, painters and mountaineers to seek the darksome, dripping, snow-dusted woods in such wild, woeful weather." Keith contains a poem, whose appearance is momentarily expected, which fact explains the waving rhythm of his prose. His storm advice was followed, and we speedily found ourselves beneath a sugar-pine roof and around a blazing fire. After partaking of a grotesque supper, Keith showed us to rooms in the abandoned hotel here, with a fine display of obsequious smiles and good-nights. It was a wild, tempestuous night; rain alternated with wind-driven hail and snow, and vivid lightning flashes seemed completely to fill the river canyon beneath, and the thunder rolled in heavy-rounded reverberations from cliff to cliff in grand accord.

A WINTRY SCENE—MOUNTAIN PLANTS

Next morning the mountains far and near were white as winter, and the forests, rising in snowy ranks, shone resplendent with the snow lodged in their dark green foliage. No tree in the Sierra forests seems to enjoy snow so much as the sugar pine. It spreads its giant arms into the welcome storm and gathers the crystal benefaction with absolute enthusiasm. The ferns and flowers were mostly buried; here and there a green, feathery frond appearing above the lavish snow-bloom, with a tall, wandy grass tuft. Not a violet or gilia to be seen. A few of the rare California Cypridpedium grows here.[2] They weathered the storm bravely. Not so the Mariposa tulip.[3] The hailstones broke

2. An apparent reference to the Sierra rein orchid (*Habenaria dilatata.*)

3. The reference is probably to the Leichtin's Mariposa tulip (*Calochortus leichtlini*), more common known as the Mariposa lily, found around Crane Flat and other open areas from middle elevations to timberline.

their wide-open corollas and bent their slender stalks. The blue
penstimon fared hardly better, and all the finest gardens, with
lark-spurs and columbines seemed hopelessly ruined. Fortunately the big Washington lily was not yet in flower, and but few
of the bush eriogonums. It would seem as if nature were dealing
but harshly with her tender plant children, as if she sought to
destroy them. Yet all that we call destruction is creating, and it is
just where storms fall most violently that the greatest quantity of
beauteous, joyous life appear. These Sierra gardens and forests
have been stormed upon for tens of thousands of years, yet we
see the upshot of all their long continued violence in the tender
and exquisite loveliness that fills them to-day.

THE GLACIAL PERIOD

Could we have visited this Yosemite region during the glacial
epoch, we would have found only fathomless wastes of ice, with
not one hint of the glorious landscapes that were being sculptured in the silence and darkness beneath, nor of the gardens and
green meadows and glad sun-born pines. Yet the glaciers were
the implements of all this lavish predestined beauty—plowing
the slates, and granite to flowing hill and dale, dome and ridge;
grinding the rocks to soil, and spreading it out in long curving
moraines and broad fielded beds. And since the planting of the
first hardy pines and frost-enduring sedges there has been a constant development toward higher and yet higher beauty. We are
camped on the right lateral moraine of the Yosemite trunk glacier, which flowed through and out of the valley with a current
over 2,000 feet in depth, and the excellence of the sugar pines
and firs, many of them over 200 feet high, without a decayed
fibre, shows how perfect is nature's system of forestry.

THE SIERRA IN JUNE

June is too early to make excursions into the high Sierra, not
only because of the frequency of small rain and snow storms,
but because feed for animals is scarce. July, August, September
and October are better months, being made up chiefly of pure
uninterrupted sunshine. Yet June snows are not greatly to be
feared. They disappear in the sun as if by magic. Yesterday the

flowers were buried, and the woods were in universal snow-bloom; to-day not a flake or hailstone is to be seen, and not a cloud in the sky. Bees drone and zigzag from flower to flower. A ruby humming bird is within a foot of my hand as I write, sipping from the purple tubes of the Menzies penstemon.[4] More than fifty butterflies have winged past me in half an hour, all dry and vigorous, and a gray squirrel is at this moment sitting on his haunches two rods distant, pulling down the seeded pods of a rock-cress with his paws, and nibbling them on the spot, like a bear eating manzanita berries.

MOUNTAIN STREAMS—SUMMER SNOW LINE

Cascade creek goes brawling by, pouring from pool to pool with its waters, more than doubled by the melting snow. Yosemite falls are no doubt similarly increased, which will be a fine thing for tourists.

The lowest point reached by the snow was about 5,500 feet above the level of the sea. Since morning this summer snow line has receded more than a thousand feet. The breaking up of the storm last evening was a most brilliant affair. The empty clouds changed to purple and pure snowy white, shot through and through with the sun, and the dripping trees were laden with flashing, irised crystals that burned on every leaf. The clouds moved hither and thither, now down among the canyon rocks, now up among the rejoicing forests, as if reviewing their accomplished work. But my letter must be closed. To-morrow we ride through many a mile of silver fir,[5] cross Yosemite creek two miles above where it leaps down into the valley and before sunset we will be camped at Lake Tenaya, one of the brightest glacier lakes in this whole Merced region.

GENTRY'S STATION,[6]
JUNE 17, 1875

4. Probably the meadow penstemon (*Penstemon heterodoxus*), which blooms in summer near subalpine meadows.

5. The nomenclature of many Sierra trees has changed over the last century. Muir is probably here referring to the white fir (*Abies concolor*), as silver firs do not grow in California.

6. Gentry's was a stagecoach stopover on the Big Oak Flat wagon road.

The high country trip made with his friends William Keith, John
Swett, and J. B. McChesney ended at Mono Lake, California, and it
was there that Muir composed the following letter, "In Sierra Forests." Muir wrote one other article near this time, but it was either
not completed or not sent to the *Bulletin*.[1]

Muir thoroughly enjoyed the forests of the northern Yosemite and
the opportunity to show them off to his close friends and to the
readers of his letters. Sights, sounds, and sensations are lovingly
presented. One of Muir's subjects, the fir-branch beds, may cause
modern readers some wonder: how could Muir indulge himself in this
practice of stripping tree branches for beds, particularly in a subalpine area where vegetation is scarce? But it must be remembered it
was these very trips which were leading Muir to his conservationist
ethic, and it was precisely these actions that led to his questioning
how man was treating his forests. It was because he reflected upon
the impact of his own actions that he became self-conscious about
some of them; indeed, the next fall he would refuse to send Mrs.
Carr a bouquet of heather, telling her he was "more and more made
to feel that my gardens and herbariums and woods are all in their
places as they grow, and I know them there, and can find them when
I will."[2] Clearly the need for a conservation policy, both personal
and national, was slowly forming in Muir's mind during these summer
trips.

Yet what most strikes the reader of Muir's letter is his unfeigned
affection for plant and animal life of all kinds. Each species is
individually appraised. Each one becomes the focus of his esteem. In
the following letter which Muir knew was destined to be a public
document, he declares the glad news that the wilderness sustains body
and soul alike, makes travelers "wholly free," and provides a place
to escape from the "cares and money" of civilization, giving man
instead a place to worship in "deep pervading repose and stillness,"
something for which Muir knew his countrymen yearned.

1. The notes on which this article would have been based can be found in
Wolfe, *John of the Mountains*, pp. 205–7.

2. Badè, *Life and Letters*, 2:54.

In Sierra Forests

Going to the mountains is going home, and gladly we climbed higher, higher, through the freshened piney woods—over meadows, over streamlets, over waving ridge and dome. It was on the morning of the 18th of June that we set out for the summits, from the top of Yosemite walls. The exhilarating snow-storm of the 15th and 16th being then fully completed and out of sight, as if it had never been—coming and going like a pleasant winter dream. The pine trees shook their tassels dry in the sun, every individual needle tingling and shimmering as if possessed of a separate life. All the mountain voices—birds, winds and leaping, plashing brooks—were tuned to downright gladness. Even our melancholy pack-mule seemed to catch a trace of the general joy as he trudged along the winding trail, heaped and humped like a dromedary with his heavy, bulging load.

The toning spiciness and richness of these forests after rain can never be described. The flowers, and buds, and leaves of every thing that grows are steeped and made into tea. Pines, with their sugar and gum and rosin; firs, with spicy balsam; pungent spruces and junipers; mossy bogs and flowery meadows, all soaked together as if in one pot, fairly filling the sky with a subtle, invigorating aroma.

We followed the Mono trail[3] around the north Yosemite wall, over the massive rounded ridge whose glacier-broken end forms the famous El Capitan; across Yosemite creek, two miles above the precipice where it leaps into the valley, along the south flank of the Hoffmann range, past Lake Tenaya, up the Big Tuolumne Meadows, past Mounts Dana and Gibbs, and down Bloody canyon to Mono.

MAGNIFICENT FORESTS

Throughout all this glorious region there is nothing that so constantly interests and challenges the admiration of the traveler

3. The Mono Trail followed a route one or two miles south of today's highway (California 120). Parts of it can still be seen around Tamarack Flat Campground or along the present trails of Tuolumne Meadows. Originally an Indian route, it became known to prospectors and sheepherders and finally to tourists as

as the belts of the forest through which he passes in regular
order. From some bare commanding hilltop we are favored with
grand out-looks over miles and miles of dark green woods, not
planted in wide fielded masses, but drawn out in lace-like pat-
terns, in curves and straight lines, that cross and recross in endless variety of arrangement, with ridges and domes of bald gray
granite between them, the area of the naked rocks greatly surpassing that of the forests. Here and there a fleck of green meadow comes into view, or the sparkle of a stream, or mirror-like
gleam of a lakelet. Hooker[4] tells us that all the cedars of
Lebanon are growing upon moraine soil; so also in general terms
are all the forests of the Sierra. If after the recession of the
ancient glaciers our forests had been compelled to wait for soil
to be rusted and crumbled for them by the slow action of the
atmosphere, they would not at this date have scarce a shadow of
their present grandeur. Here and there a tree would be found
clinging to rifts in the glacial pavement, and a few groves would
find sufficient soil in shallow lake basins filled with sand, but
these luxuriant forest belts, forming the crowning glory of the
mountains, would have no existence. As it was, the glaciers furrowed the solid rocks, turning and mixing the detritus, and leaving it in just that condition most favorable for the food of
forests, and in conjunction with climate bringing about their
present magnificence as a necessary result.

Few travelers will, however, take the time to trace out the
order or distribution, or the history of the various forests, but
no one will weary in admiring special trees. *Pinus Lambertiana*
(Sugar Pine) is the acknowledged king of pines, and many a volume might be filled with the history of its development from the
brown, whirling-winged seed nut to its ripe and God-like old
age; the quantity and range of its individuality, its gestures in
storms or while sleeping in summer light, the quality of its sugar
and nut, and glossy fragrant wood.

---

they traveled to the camping areas of the Tuolumne and Mount Lyell regions of
Yosemite. The eastern terminus of the trail was Mono Lake, located at the eastern base of the Sierra.

4. Joseph Hooker, English botanist, who was to come to California two years
later and camp with Muir in the Shasta region.

There stands a specimen 250 feet high, 8 feet in diameter, with a smooth, purplish trunk exquisitely tapered, and with graceful, spreading, down-curving branches 40 feet long, terminated by cone tassels adjusted with reference to size, distribution and color, as if made for beauty only. Could such a pine be carried from its woods to wave, and sing, and toss its giant arms in some Central City park, all would flock to see it as a wonder of the world.

It is almost universally conceded by those who are so happy as to have eaten the sugar, that it is the most delicious of known sweets, far surpassing the best maple sugar. It exudes from wounds made either by fire or the ax in the heartwood, forming white, crisp, candy-like kernels from the size of peas to hazelnuts, and contains just enough of a spicy, balsamic flavor to render it pleasingly and becomingly spicy.

PINE-NUTS AND SEEDS AS FOOD

The largest full-grown cones measure about seventeen or eighteen inches in length, though one in my possession measures two feet. A single cone yields nuts enough to make a good square meal for an Indian. They climb the more accessible of the trees and beat off the cones while they are yet green, then roast them slightly, thus opening the scales and exposing the nuts; but owing to the difficulties in the way of climbing the trees and reaching out to the ends of the long branches, this nut forms but a small portion of their food. The Sabine pine[5] growing on the low foothills of the western slope furnishes larger nuts that are more readily gathered. The dwarf Fremont pine[6] growing upon the sunbeaten rocks of the eastern flank of the Sierra furnishes the Mono, Carson and Walker river Indians[7] with more and better nuts than any other tree, with the least possible exertion. This, undoubtedly, is the most important food tree of all the California coniferae. The nuts are called pinyons by the Indians, and when the harvest is abundant their joy finds expression in

5. The digger pine (*Pinus sabiniana*) grows widely in California western foothills below 4,500 feet.
6. The singleleaf pinyon (*Pinus monophylla*) ranges from 6,000' to 8,000'.
7. Members of the Paiute tribes.

long-continued nut dances similar to the acorn dances of the
Diggers. Bears also munch pine seeds with extraordinary gusto,
and know well how to tear the burrs open. To the squirrels they
are bread both winter and summer. When the large gray squirrel
wishes the nuts of the yellow pine, he glides out to the ends of
the branches, pulls back the springy needles out of his way, leans
over and cuts off the burr with his long curved teeth, carefully
holding on to it with his paws to prevent its falling, then seizing
it with grotesquely stretched jaws he carries it to some favorite
dining branch, where he can sit comfortably on his haunches.
Here he sets it on end upside down and gnaws off the seed-pro-
tecting scales round and round in regular order, his retreat being
indicated by a dribble of gnawed scales and seed wings. But the
immense size of the sugar cones compels a quite different
course. These he cuts off and lets drop to the ground without
attempting to hold them, easily harvesting in this way a sufficient number in a few minutes to last a month, then he gnaws
and nibbles them as they lie among the dead needles, rolling
them over and over as the feast goes on, like a pig eating corn
from the cob—the strongest squirrel being unable to hold them
erect in the regular orthodox manner.

THE YELLOW PINE—THE SILVER FIR—
THE HOFFMAN FOREST

The Yellow Pine,[8] the constant companion of the sugar,
stands second in importance among California pines as a lumber
tree, and almost rivals the king himself in stature and nobleness
of parts. The traveler will find it keeping him company all the
way up this middle region of the Sierra from an elevation above
sea level of 2,000 to 9,000 feet. Growing in fine spirey symmetry
upon ancient moraines, alluvial lake beds and hot volcanic table-
lands, and whether basking in light or waving and rocking in
storms, its true nobleness is always patent to the eye of the
appreciative tree lover.

At an elevation of six or seven thousand feet we find the silver

8. The ponderosa pine (*Pinus ponderosa*). It has been found as low as the
150-foot elevation in El Dorado County.

fir,[9] with flat, glistening, plume-like branches, frequently attaining a height of more than two hundred feet, and a diameter of five or six feet.

About a thousand feet higher, the place of this tree as chief of the forest is taken by a still finer silver fir,[10] but they unite and bend by a long, gradual splice, and the two form the main bulk of the forest at the elevation given above.

The Hoffmann forest, through which we rode, is one of the finest I have ever met in all my mountaineering, and our whole party were as extravagant as possible in its praise, but to be known it must be seen and lived with. Its surpassing excellence is probably owing to the depth and richness of the moraine upon which it is growing, being composed of eroded slates and granite mixed well together and toned with plenty of iron, and spread out in the sunshine, with abundance of small percolative streamlets.

THE FOREST WORK OF NATURE

Happy is the man with the will and the time to climb a silver fir in full flower and fruit. How admirable the forest work of Nature is seen to be as one ascends from branch to branch, all arranged in regular collars around the trunk, one above the other like the whorled leaves of lilies, and with each branch and branchlet about as strictly pinnate as the most exact and symmetrical fern frond. There is also the added beauty of the sterile or staminate conelets, growing straight downward from the under sides of the branches in lavish profusion, and coloring the whole tree in delightful purple. On the topmost branches are found the fertile cones six inches long, three in diameter, covered with fine grayish down, standing bolt upright like small caskets, and all dripping with delicious crystal balsam. The seeds are furnished with rose-purple wings with which to fly to their appointed growing places in the groves, and are filled with ex-

9. The white fir (*Abies concolor.*)

10. The red fir (*Abies magnifica*), whose greater flexibility enables it to survive the great snows of the higher elevations. Muir later called this tree *Picea amabilus,* although he corrected himself when using parts of this narrative in his *Mountains of California;* see "The Forests," pp. 139–225.

ceedingly pungent aromatic oil. The Douglass squirrel feeds largely on these seeds, which may account for the flashing lightning energy with which he is pervaded. Under favorable conditions the silver fir attains to venerable old age, seldom dying before approaching or exceeding two hundred and fifty years. One old parent is oftentimes seen standing apart, somewhat ruffled and scarred by centuries of storms, with a protecting circle of younglings, dressed with such perfect care that not a single leaf seems wanting. Other companies are made up of trees in the prime of life, so exquisitely adjusted to one another in form and stature as to suggest Nature's culling them one by one with the nicest discrimination from all the rest of the woods. It is from this tree (*Picea amabilis*), called "red fir" by the lumberman, that the mountaineer always cuts boughs for a bed when he is so fortunate as to be within its limits. Every twig is crowded with short elastic leaves, rendering the branches more plushy than the thickest Brussels carpet, to say nothing of their delicious balsam aroma.

Our company had never before enjoyed the rare luxury of a silver fir bed, and all confessed that no invention of hair, wool or feathers could approach it in pure softness and springy ease, only Highland heather might compare in balmy restfulness.

UNDEVELOPED FLORA—NATURE'S GRAND SOLITUDES

The flora of this fine world of ours is not yet half developed. For not to mention the innumerable small plants, the violas and daisies blooming lowly out of sight, many a tree remains nameless in nature's ample wilds. It is but a few years since the great Australian Eucalyptus was first made known to civilization,[11] and what tree treasures the untrodden Himalaya may contain we can hardly guess. But as yet our silvery Amabilis remains unrivaled among the firs of the world, and no wonder the enthusiastic Douglass[12] went wild with the joy of its discovery.

11. The eucalyptus was originally imported into California with the purpose of using its wood for railroad ties. It was unsuited for that, but large groves were planted and it is now commonly found throughout the state. One large specimen planted by Muir still stands next to his house in Martinez, California.

12. Botanist David Douglas explored the Pacific Northwest and northern California, discovering and naming numerous species of trees and animals.

Through the glorious Hoffmann wilderness we sauntered
wholly free. The day was perfect sunshine, and in the coolest,
deepest shades there was no trace of the dampness and swampi-
ness so common in thrifty woods. Sun-gold streamed through
many an opening and fell on the smooth ground as on a canvass
in bars and lakes of light. The deep pervading repose and stillness was stirred only by cascading water and by the drumming
partridges and garrulous stellar jay.[13] How perfect was the obliv-
ion that fell upon the fever-work of the far off towns. Even
Yosemite, along whose rim we rode, was almost forgotten; nothing of its rocks or falls being seen, and nothing to tell of its existence, excepting only the lofty Half Dome which rose impressively above the woods wherever we went and made its mark on
every landscape. Nothing about Yosemite creek is so striking as
the simplicity and clearness of its beauty. No one of all the
streams that leap Yosemite walls lives so subdued and tranquil a
life. Whether flowing around level bends, through leafy margin
groves, or leaping rocky dams, or cascading adown glacier
slopes, it still seems to be checking itself as if hoarding back all
its best talents, conscious of its sublime work in leading the
Yosemite choir. Where it is crossed by the Mono trail, some two
miles from the brink of the valley, it is a handsome stream three
feet deep and thirty wide, flowing with a rippling current over
brown pebbles, between grassy banks adorned with dipping willows and patches of spiraea and azalea, all in bloom. Back a
little distance there are level sandy flats, rosetted with spragnea
and hazy with purple gilias, and beyond are domes in endless
variety, bare and shining as if glaciated only yesterday.

LAKE TENAYA—A SYLVAN EDEN

From the top of a hill 700 feet high we catch our first glimpse
of Lake Tenaya—a goblet of sparkling mountain water, blue
and pure as the sky. Here, some twenty-five years ago, the plun-
dering Indians fled from Yosemite, pursued by Captain Savage's
volunteers, and the fine lake perpetuates the old chief's (Tenaya)

13. The blue grouse (*Dedragapus obscurus*) is commonly found in the red fir
forests; the males produce a "booming" sound during the mating season. The
Steller's jay (*Cyanocitta stelleri*) is among the most conspicuous of the Sierra
birds.

"Cathedral Peak Group—Upper Tuolumne Valley." Engraving by John Andrews. From Whitney, *Yosemite Guide Book.*

name. It measures about a mile in length, and is encompassed by glaciated domes and mountains, whose smoothness and glistening brightness strike the dullest observer with admiration. Mount Hoffmann rises in full view on the north, Colisieum Peak on the south and Cathedral Peak on the east, with numerous domes and waves of glacier's polished granite flowing down to the water's edge in graceful folds like drapery. We have no space here to tell of the marvelous beauty of the water in the changing lights of morning and evening, or of the ancient Mer de Glace, whose ice-floods filled all its basin and flowed above its domes. Along its glossy shores we rode with many a tribute of praise, and were soon out of sight in the woods, and on our way to the Big Tuolumne meadows, lying some six or seven miles to the eastward of the lake. In these higher woods we find the burly brown barked juniper, eight feet in diameter, covered with berries and growing upon pure unbroken granite. The wood of this tree furnishes the fragrant cedar of the pencil makers. Here, too, we find the noble mountain pine, living happily above reach of the lumberman's axe, and in the coolest mountain shadows, where the winter snow falls deepest, we discover the Williamson spruce, the most singularly graceful tree of all the Sierra coniferae.[14] So slender is its axis at the top, it bends over and droops like the stalk of a nodding lily. The branches are divided into slender drooping sprays and are put on and combined in a manner that is wholly indescribable. The purple cones are sprinkled over the bluish green foliage from top to bottom, and the whole tree is a poem, not a single prose leaf, or branch, or motion, is ever visible. No tree in all the woods is so slender and delicate, and excepting the flexible pine no other is so heavily crushed beneath the winter snow. In my winter walks I have found whole groves of this abies prostrate as stalks of grass or wind-lodged wheat. But this is nature's culture—her system of bedding—of putting to winter sleep; and when the spring comes with its sunshine, these heavy snow blankets are lifted, and her favorite

14. The western white pine (*Pinus monticola*), also known as silver pine. The "Williamson spruce" is not native to California, and Muir is here describing the mountain hemlock (*Tsuga mertensiana*) with its characteristic drooping top.

spruces rise again to wave and lave in the warm azure more delicately beautiful than before.

TUOLUMNE MEADOWS

Out of the forest shadows, through clusters of glacier domes, we all at once emerge into the wide roomy meadows of the Upper Tuolumne. The mountains here seem to have been cleared away to make room for them, for they stand thick around its sides, rising sharp and gray above the sombre forests that clothe their flanks. The meadows are smooth and green, and nearly fifteen miles long, with the Young Tuolumne like a ribbon in their midst, and curving around and up to the very base of Mount Lyell on the summit of the range. On our right, as we enter the meadows, stands Cathedral Peak, a very temple of nature—a church of one stone, cut from the living granite, hewn and chiseled in a human way, and adorned with spires and pinnacles in front, with dwarf pines, like mosses, on the roof and around the edges of the gable, as if nature were a common workman with human tastes and methods.

SODA SPRINGS—GRAND CAMPING GROUND

Two miles from where we enter the meadows we find the Soda Springs well known to every Indian and mountaineer of the region. The water is icy soda, toned with iron and a little sulphur and magnesia, forming a very wholesome and refreshing drink, just as cold as can be freely drank (46 deg. Fah.), and fully charged with carbonic acid. This undoubtedly is one of the most important mineral springs in the State, and if more accessible would be thronged with health-pleasure seekers from far and near. I am not acquainted with any point in the High Sierra adjacent to Yosemite so advantageous and desirable for a central camping ground to those who have a summer to spend. Visits can be made to Mount Dana and to Mount Lyell with its living glacier, to the head of the great Tuolumne canyon, to the glacier monument, to Mount Conness, Unicorn Peak, Cathedral Peak, and the North Tuolumne Church. All these lie within easy distance of the springs with many points and objects of interest besides, as avalanche pathways, glacier channels, glacier lakes

and meadows, etc. All these, with delicious air and water, where
one gets his boyhood back again, and where morbid hopes and
morbid fears, either for this life or any other, are alike forgotten, and the sick get well. Let those contemplating health
journeys to fashionable Bethesdas bear Tuolumne in mind.

MONO PASS—DWARF PINES—ANIMAL LIFE

On the third morning from Gentry's we set out from the
Springs to the summit of the Mono Pass, ten miles distant, and
nearly 11,000 feet above the level of the sea. Here we made our
noon halt by a pretty lakelet among arctic willows and daisies,
preparatory to descending the famous Bloody Canyon.[15] This is
about the upper limits of the timber line formed by the hardy
pinus flexilis,[16] which covers the bleak mountain sides in many
places like heather, over the top of which we can easily walk.
Though some of these dwarfy pines, shorn and repressed by rig-
orous storm-winds, scarcely exceed three feet in height, they frequently reach the good old age of two hundred years. One slim
branch that I examined, measuring only a little over an eighth of
an inch in diameter inside the bark, was seventy-five years old,
and was so seasoned in storms that I tied it into knots like a
cord. The staminate cones grow in close sessile clusters, and are
bright rose-purple in color, producing a fine effect, little looked
for in such a tree. The fertile cones are also produced in close-
packed clusters, on the ends of the upper branches, and bear
seeds about the size of peas, and nearly as round and white as
hailstones. Most of the nuts are eaten by the sparrow-squirrel
(*Tamias*), and the notable Clark crow (*picicornaas*),[17] the most

15. There are two Mono Passes in the Sierra; the one Muir describes (10,604')
is found just south of Mount Gibbs. The famous "Bloody Canyon" was the
topic of a Muir article published the previous fall. See his "By-Ways of Yosemite
Travel: Bloody Cañon," *Overland Monthly* 13 (September 1874): 267–73.

16. Muir made a marginal notation on his copy of this letter changing *Pinus
flexilis* to *Albicaulis,* and it is this tree, called whitebark pine, which he meant to
identify in the article.

17. Muir's "Tamias" is perhaps the pika (*Ochotona princeps*), or more likely
the Sierra Nevada golden-mantled ground squirrel (*Calospermophilus lateralis*);
the *picicornaas* is the loud, large "Clark's nutcracker" (*Nucifraga columbiana*),
familiar to all travelers in the high Sierra.

garrulous and omnipresent bird of the high summits. He is a little larger than a jay, wearing black and ash colored plumage, and with a bill pointed like a miner's pick for digging into the pine-burrs. The little dun-headed Arctic sparrow[18] is here also, and finds his food still higher, feeding chiefly upon beetles and butterflies that become chilled in attempting to cross the snow-fields and glaciers. Upon these banks of perpetual ice and snow his food is thus spread for him as upon a clean white cloth, and a more confiding and cheery little fellow was never seen. Amid these glorious Alps, San Francisco, with its cares and money, became yet more perfectly invisible. Swett forgot his new-born lassie, Mack forgot his son, and Keith all but his paints and pencils.

Mono Lake,
July 1875

18. The gray-crowned rosy finch (*Leucostichte tephrocotis*), the hardiest of all mountain-dwelling birds.

PART THREE
To Kings Canyon and Mount Whitney's Summit

By which it appears that all the
destructible beauty of this remote
Yosemite is doomed to perish like
that of its neighbors, and our tame
law-loving citizens plant and water
their garden daisies without concern,
wholly unconscious of loss.

August 1875

John Muir had completed his major glacial investigations by the fall
of 1875 with the writing of a series of articles entitled "Studies in the
Sierra," published in the *Overland Monthly*. Free at last from this
task, and with his "Yosemite Book" at least planned if not completed, he began other scientific investigations. These new studies
would shift his travels from the glacial fountains of the high peaks
down into the sequoia forests of the Kings Canyon and Kaweah
Divide and into the ancient moraines formed on the western Sierra
slopes. Muir recorded his wilderness wanderings and his scientific
findings in the letter-articles to the *Bulletin* which are reprinted
below.

One discovery he made (and plainly his previous wanderings had
led him to it) was how few people knew to what degree the state's
forests were endangered. The groves were disappearing not so much
through the lumbering operations he saw at work, but primarily because of the forest fires deliberately set by sheepmen. These annual
fires were set in order to clear out the forest underbrush and to
permit the flocks easier pathways to the high meadow pasturage, and
Muir, angered by what he saw, would appeal to his readers to con-
demn the practice. The *Bulletin* letters which follow contain the first
hints of this kind of message. Muir returned from these trips with a

new resolve, and while in the next few years he continued to wander
up and down the Sierra in his private study of the state's forests, he
was also preparing himself to become their protector. This meant, of
course, that he would have to become a member of the very community he was disposed to criticize. Muir did this, although he
claimed to do so only reluctantly. He spent the winter of 1874–75 in
Oakland and San Francisco with friends, and these men and women
—people like Ina Coolbrith the poet, William Keith, Professors
Joseph LeConte and Ezra Carr, and the radical reformer Henry
George—gave Muir a wider perspective on why and how he might
correct the wrongs he perceived to exist.

The three letters to the *Bulletin* reprinted in this next part give
detailed descriptions of a Sierra region few people had seen. While
his articles are full of scientific notations on the geology and plants
of the region, and record for us a wilderness area no longer wild and
a wilderness experience not possible to recreate, they may also be
simply enjoyed as records of camping and traveling not unlike those
described in the earlier journals of William Brewer and Clarence
King. Throughout these passages are Muir's perspective and voice,
leading his readers from discovery to discovery, picturing each day as
more fresh and exhilarating than the one before.

A New Yosemite—The King's River Valley

Nature is seldom suspected of being poor, for does she not
possess all the real estate of the world, to say nothing of un-
explored moons and stars? and has she then only one Yosemite
Valley? It is now nearly a quarter of a century since the Indians
were first disturbed by the intrusion of the whites into this their
finest mountain home and stronghold, and though all sorts of
people have written of the grandeur and loveliness of its rocks
and snowy waters, the world at large remains strangely blind to
the fact, that in the Sierra Nevada there are many Yosemites,
differing from this one in no other way or degree than one man
or mountain differs from another. Ever since its discovery we
have been assured by scientists that Yosemite stood alone and
unrelated among all the known valleys of the world. There was

nothing like it in Switzerland; in the recesses of the snow-capped Andes; in the Himalaya, or Africa's Mountains of the Moon. It was a special church or temple in which all the landscape-loving world should do extraordinary worship. Or according to other penmen perhaps scarcely less devout, it was to be regarded as a mere geological marvel on a grand scale, which like ancient miracles, lay at a hopeless distance beyond the boundaries of exact science, the very grandeur and simplicity of its forms preventing the recognition of the plain truth that it constitutes one harmonious and natural feature of the noble mountain landscape in which it lies. Some three years ago I called public attention to Hetch Hetchy Valley, situated on the Tuolumne river twelve miles in an air line to the northwest of here, showing at the same time that in every essential particular it was a Yosemite valley, formed by the same forces, lying at the same height above sea level, occupying the same relative position on the flank of the range, and its lofty granite walls sculptured and wrought into the same species of sublime forms, and the whole adorned and inspired with the same kinds and combinations of plants and waterfalls.[1]

THE NEW YOSEMITE

I have just returned from an extended excursion to the summit of Mount Whitney, in the course of which I passed through the King's[2] river Yosemite, which is larger, and in some respects more interesting than the Yosemites of the Tuolumne and Merced. This magnificent valley is situated upon the South Fork of King's river, about forty-five miles from Visalia in a straight line. It measures about nine miles in length from east to west, and has an average width at bottom of about half a mile. The walls are quite as precipitous as those of Yosemite, so-called,

1. Muir composed this article at the conclusion of the trip to Kings Canyon. His claim to priority in publicizing Hetch Hetchy is based on his "Hetch-Hetchy Valley," *Overland Monthly* 10 (July 1873): 42–50. This is of course the same valley which Muir fought to save during the early 1900s.
2. There was some confusion during Muir's time over the spellings of many Sierra landmarks. What Muir styled "King's" is now "Kings," from the Spanish *Los Reyes* (a plural, not possessive, form).

"Three Sisters" (sequoia trees). Engraving by Thomas Armstrong. In Hutchings, *Scenes of Wonder and Curiosity in California*, p. 49. Courtesy the Bancroft
Library.

and are about three thousand feet in height, and sculptured into the same noble forms that characterize all the Yosemites of the Sierra.[3] The bottom of the valley is about 5,000 feet above the level of the sea, and its level surface is diversified with meadows and groves, through which the river pours its crystal floods in lavish abundance—now calmly and with scarce a ripple over the brown pebbles and sheets of yellow sand, now in rushing rapids over beds of mossy bowlders and dams of avalanche debris.

We set out from here [Yosemite Valley] on the 9th of July, our party consisting of George Bayley of San Francisco, Charles Washburn,[4] a student of the State University, with "Buckskin Bill" as mule master, all well mounted on tough, obstinate mules. Right gladly we pushed our way into the wild untrampled kingdoms of the Sierra, inspired with the thousand indefinite joys of the green summer woods; past Clark's Station[5] and the Mariposa Grove of Big Trees; through the luxuriant forests of the Upper Fresno, fairly dripping with balsam and gum; climbing many a hill and dale bestrewn with brown burs, and fording

3. Muir is here using the term "yosemite" to refer to all the glacial carved valleys of the Sierra. He also often employed the adjective "Yosemitic" to describe characteristic rock formations commonly found in the Sierra valleys. Muir's emphasis on the glacial origin of the Kings River Canyon was overstated. Recent geologic interpretation suggests the canyon was formed almost exclusively through water erosion. Glacial action was not the dominant actor in its creation primarily because the ancient ice flows in this portion of the Sierra were much smaller than those in the Yosemite region.

4. George Bayley is described by Muir as "a firm, condensed, muscular little man who comes aclimbing in the mountains every year. His love of alpine exercise seems to suffer no abatement, notwithstanding he scrambles most of the year among the dangerous heights and hollows of the San Francisco stock market. He a short man, or even shorter." (*Bulletin* of September 6, 1876.) Bayley was a pioneer of Mount Rainier climbs and the first to ascend Mount Starr King. His life is described in Evelyn H. Chase, *Mountain Climber: George B. Bayley, 1840–1894* (Palo Alto: Pacific Books, 1981). Charles Washburn graduated from the University of California the year following the events recorded here; he died in 1884. See Francis P. Farquhar, *History of the Sierra Nevada* (Berkeley: University of California Press, 1965), p. 187n.

5. Galen Clark, first Guardian of the Yosemite Grant, had opened his Wawona Station in the 1860s; it was a frequent stopover for visitors entering the Yosemite from Fresno or who wished to stay near the Mariposa Grove of sequoias.

many a bright dashing brook hedged with tangled alders and willows; making a devious trail, yet tending ever southward, independent in our course as birds in the calm cloudless air. Soon we found ourselves among the heated foothills of the San Joaquin, and on the edge of the strangely dappled plains. At Centreville we crossed the wide stately current of King's river, still transparent and sparkling as if fresh from its high Alpine snows, then facing eastward climbed to the piney woods again, and meandered like a headless river through the magnificent groves of King Sequoias that still flourish in cool glens and hollows from King's river southward to the Kaweah, and yet beyond. Here we heard the sound of axes, and soon came upon a group of busy men engaged in preparing a butt section of a giant sequoia they had felled for exhibition at the Quaker Centennial.[6] This tree was twenty-five feet in diameter at the base, and so fine was the taper of the trunk that it still measured ten feet in diameter at a height of two hundred feet from the ground. According to the testimony of the annual wood-rings counted by three different persons, this tree at the time of its death was from 2,125 to 2,317 years old. The section cut for exhibition is 16 feet long, split into eight immense staves, the heartwood being removed by splitting and hewing until the staves measure about eight inches in thickness inside the bark. When therefore the section is set up for exhibition it will appear as a huge tub cut from a hollow log. The speculative genius who planned and is executing this sequoia enterprise is Martin Vivian of Helena, Montana, and in order to make the most of it, he purposes placing his rustic tub on exhibition during the coming winter in St. Louis. A wagon road has been graded into the grove, and the staves are now almost ready for transportation to the railroad.

Many a poor, defrauded town dweller will pay his dollar and peep, and gain some dead arithmetical notion of the bigness of our Big Trees, but a true and living knowledge of these tree gods

6. So-called because the 1876 Centennial celebration was to be held in Philadelphia. The remains of the tree Muir here describes, now called the "Centennial stump," rest in the Grant Grove area of Kings Canyon National Park. Other examples of reconstructed trees—made barrel fashion from bark staves—were displayed at the Smithsonian and in London.

is not to be had at so cheap at rate. As well try to send a section of the storms on which they feed.

A GLORIOUS VIEW

Out of this solemn ancient forest we climbed, still upward and eastward, into the cool realms of the Alpine pines, and at length caught a long, sweeping view of the beetling cliffs and rock brows that form the walls of the glorious Yosemite, for which we were so eagerly looking. The trail by which we descended to the bottom of the valley enters at the lower or west end, zigzagging in a wild independent fashion over the South Lip, and corresponding in a general way both in position and direction to the Mariposa trail of the Merced Yosemite, and like it, affording a series of enchanting views up the valley, over the groves and meadows between the massive granite walls. Indeed, so fully and radically were these views Yosemitic in all their leading features it was difficult to realize that we were not entering the old Yosemite by Inspiration Point. Bayley's joy usually finds expression in a kind of explosive Indian war whoop, and wild echoes were driven rudely from cliff to cliff, as the varied landscapes revealed themselves from the more commanding points along the trail.

BOTTOM OF THE VALLEY—A SIERRA FLOWER-GARDEN

In about two hours after beginning the descent, we found ourselves among the sugar pine groves at the lower end of the valley, through which we rode in perfect ecstasy, for never did pines seem so noble and religious in all their gestures and tones. The sun pouring down mellow gold, seemed to be shining only for them, and the wind gave them voice, but the gestures of their outstretched arms appeared wholly independent of the winds, and impressed one with a solemn awe that overbore all our knowledge of causes and brought us into the condition of beings new-arrived from some other far off world. The ground was smoothly strewn with dead, clean leaves and burs, making a fine brown surface for shadows, many a wide, even bar, from tapering trunk columns, and rich mosaic from living leaf and branch. There amid the groves we came to small openings without a tree or shadow, wholly filled with the sun, like pools of glowing light. We camped on the river-bank a mile or two up the valley near a small circular meadow, that is one of the most perfect and downright flower-gardens I have ever discovered in the mountains. The trampling mules, whom I would fain have kept out, fairly disappeared beneath the broad, overarching ferns that encircled the garden proper. It was filled with lilies and violets, and orchards,[7] and sun-loving golden rods and asters, and oenothera, and purple geraniums, and epilobium,[8] with a hundred others all in bloom, but whose names no one would read, though all the world would love to revel in their beauty as they grow. One of the tiger lilies that I measured was six feet long, and had eleven open flowers, five of them in prime beauty. The wind rocked this splendid orange panicle above the heads of the geraniums and brier roses, forming a spectacle of pure beauty exquisitely poised and harmonized in all its parts. It was as if nature had fingered every leaf and petal that very day, readjusting every curve, and touching the colors of every corolla; and so she had, for not a leaf was misbent, and every plant was so placed with reference to every other in form and color that the whole garden had evidently been arranged like one tasteful bouquet. Here I lived a fine unmeasured hour "considering the lilies," warming among the mellow waving golden rods, and gazing into the countenances of the briars and small white violets. Every individual flower radiated beauty as real and appreciable as sunbeams, and the lily bells swinging on their long stalks rang out music that was heard as plainly as the river, or wind in the pine tops. Many other wild gardens occur along the river bank, and in cool side dells where a stream comes out of a canyon, but neither at this time nor during my former visit to the Valley were any discovered so perfect as this one. The lower half of the Valley consists of sugar-pine groves divided by sunny park-like openings on which manzanita and several species of ceonothus form a scanty covering. Some of these openings are

7. This is probably a mistyping in the *Bulletin* of "orchards" for "orchids." Muir evidently was referring to the Sierra rein orchid.

8. *Oenothera:* primrose. *Epilobium:* possibly the "rock fringe," *Epilobium obcordatum.*

dry and gravelly and grow fine crops of Monardella for the bees, together with Eriogonae and the most sun-loving Compositae[9] for butterfly and humming bird pastures. Towards the upper end of the valley there is quite an extensive meadow that reaches from wall to wall.[10] The river bank, groves and borders are made up chiefly of Alder, Poplar, and Willow, and a rich measure of Azalea, Brier Rose and Wild Honeysuckle, all combined with reference to the best beauty, and to the special wants of the wide crystal river.

THE WALLS—NATURE REPEATING HERSELF

Beginning at the lower end of the valley, the first two miles of the walls are leveled off at the tops, and are so broken and soil-besprinkled they support quite a number of trees and shaggy bushes, but farther up the granite speedily assumes Yosemitic forms and dimensions, rising in stupendous cliffs, angular and sheer from the level flats and meadows. On the north wall there is an El Capitan and group of Three Brothers. Farther up on the same side there is an Indian Canyon and North Dome and Washington Column. On the south wall counterparts of the Sentinel and Cathedral Rocks occur in regular order bearing the same relative position to one another that they do in the old Yosemite, for the simple reason that like causes produce like effects, both valleys being in general terms simple pieces of erosion accomplished by the ancient glaciers that flowed through them.

WATERFALLS

With regard to waterfalls, those of the Old Yosemite are more striking and impressive in their forms and in the songs they sing, although the whole quantity of water that pours over the walls is considerably less and comes from lower sources. The waters of the new valley effect their descent by a series of comparatively short leaps and inclines, which, according to the vague classifi-

9. Members of the sunflower family. Those commonly found at high altitudes are the "cut-leaved daisy" (*Erigeron compositus*) and "Sierra daisy" (*E. petiolarus*).

10. Zumwalt Meadows, elevation 5,035'.

cation in vogue in these dark, pretentious days, would mostly be brought under the head of cascades. These, however, are exceedingly beautiful, more beautiful than vertical falls, and belong to a higher type of water beauty. Nevertheless, it may be long ere waterfalls have their beauty measured in any other way than by plumb-lines and tape-lines.

AN ENCHANTING RIDE—WONDERFUL VIEWS

Our ride up the Valley was perfectly enchanting, every bend of the river presenting reaches of surpassing loveliness, sunbeams streaming through its border groves, or falling in broad masses upon the white rapids or calm, deep pools. Here and there a dead pine that had been swept down in flood time reached out over the current, its green mosses and lichens contrasting with the crystal sheen of the water, and its gnarled roots forming shadowy caves for speckled trout where the current eddies slowly, and protecting edges and willows dip their leaves. Among these varied and ever-changing river reaches the appreciative artist may find studies for a lifetime.

The deeply sculptured walls presented more and more exciting views, calling forth the unbounded admiration of the whole party. Bold sheer brows standing forth into a full blaze of light, deep shadowy side gorges and canyons inhabited by wild cascades, groups of gothic gables, glacier-polished domes, coming into view in ever-changing combinations, and with different foregrounds. Yet no individual rock in the valley equals El Capitan or Half Dome, but, on the other hand, from no position on the Yosemite walls could a section five miles in length be selected equal in downright beauty and grandeur to five miles of the middle portion of the south wall of the new valley.

We camped for the night at the foot of the new Washington column,[11] where the ferns and lilies reached to our heads, their rich, lavish exuberance contrasting strikingly with the massive, naked walls.

The summer day died in purple and gold, and we lay watching the growing shadows and the fading sunglow among the heights.

11. Present name: the Sentinel. Elevation, 8,504′.

Each member of the party made his own bed, like birds building nests. Mine was made of fern fronds, with a sprinkling of mint spikes in the pillow, thus combining luxurious softness with delicate fragrance, in which one sleeps not only restfully but deliciously, making the down beds of palaces and palace hotels seem poor and vulgar by contrast.

THE NEW VALLEY AT NIGHT

The full moon rose just after the night darkness was fairly established. The dim gray cliff at the foot of which we lay was crowned with an arch of white, cold light long before the moon's disc appeared above the opposite wall. Down the valley one rock-front after another caught the silvery glow, and came out from the gray and dusky shadows in long, imposing ranks, like very spirits, forming altogether one of the most impressive scenes I ever beheld. The tranquil sky was also intensely lovely, blooming with stars like a meadow, and the thickets and groves along the river banks were masses of solid darkness. It was too surpassingly beautiful a night for sleep, and we feasted long upon the rare scene ere the weariness of enjoyment closed our eyes. Next morning we rode up the valley in the sunshine, follow-the north bank of the river to where it forks at the head. The glacier-polished rocks glowed in the slant sunbeams in many places as if made of burnished steel. All the glacial phenomena of the new valley, the polished surfaces, roches montanees, and moraines, are fresher and less changed than those of the old. It is evidently a somewhat younger valley, a fact easily explained by its relations to the fountains of the ancient glaciers lying above it in the snowy Alps. Like the old valley, this also is a favorite summer resort of Indians, because it produces acorns and its streams abound in trout, and, no doubt, they have names for all the principal rocks and cascades, and possess numerous grotesque and ornamental legends, though as yet I have not been able to learn any of them. A good mountain trail conducts out of the head of the valley, across the range by the Kearsarge Pass to Owens Valley, which we followed, and reached Independence in two days, where we made up our outfit for the ascent of Mt. Whitney, the loftiest peak in the range.

HOW TO GET THERE—PRIMEVAL HOG PASTURE

This new King's river Yosemite is already beginning to attract tourists from all parts of the world, and its fame will soon equal that of the old. It is quite as accessible, the distance from the railroad being, as we have said, only about 45 miles in an airline, and the greater portion of the distance is by a good wagon road. Horses and all the necessary outfit may be obtained at Visalia, and the excursion has the advantage of comprehending the finest groves of big trees in the State, as well as a section of the best pine and fir forests, and if the trail be followed to Independence, views will be had of the very highest portion of the Sierra. The Kearsarge Pass is over 12,000 feet in height, and is located in the midst of a perfect wilderness of peaks from 13,000 to over 14,000 feet in height, rising from rare glacial meadows and lakes, and adorned around their bases by a multitude of the very dearest of Alpine flowers.

Those who can should visit the valley at once, while it remains in primeval order. Some twenty-five years ago the Tuolumne Yosemite [Hetch Hetchy Valley] was made into a hog pasture, and later into a sheep pasture. The Merced Yosemite has all its wild gardens trampled by cows and horses, and we noticed upon a pine tree in the King's river Valley the following inscription:

"We the undersigned claim this valley for the purpose of raising stock, etc.

MR. THOMAS,
"   RICHARD,
"   HARVEY & CO."

By which it appears that all the destructible beauty of this remote Yosemite is doomed to perish like that of its neighbors, and our tame law-loving citizens plant and water their garden daisies without concern, wholly unconscious of loss.

YOSEMITE VALLEY,
AUGUST 5, 1875

Muir left Kings Canyon by walking east up the Bubbs Creek trail and over Kearsarge Pass, to arrive a short time later in the small town of Independence, California. Here he made immediate plans to take his companions on a climb of the nation's highest peak.

Two years before, Muir had been among the first half-dozen to ascend Mount Whitney, and he remained the only climber to have gone up the difficult eastern route. He describes this hike in the following letter, entitled "Mount Whitney." Muir presents some interesting glimpses into a style of mountaineering, and throughout the letter defends the *art* of climbing, suggesting in one instance that mountains are never "conquered." This attitude is in stark contrast to the prevalent practice and philosophy of climbing during the times, perhaps best exemplified by Clarence King. King's relationship with Muir, never a warm one, deteriorated rapidly after the appearance of this letter, partly because of the men's disagreement over geological matters, partly because of King's mistakes and Muir's account of them in the conclusion of this letter. King, a member of Josiah Whitney's Geological Survey Party, after discovering Mount Whitney in 1863, had made two failed attempts to reach its summit, and in 1870 attempted a third climb. Walking up a peak lying some six miles to the south of Whitney (today known as Mount Langley) and thinking he had "conquered" the highest mountain, he wrote an exaggerated account of the climb for the *Atlantic Monthly.* But in 1872 his error was announced before the California Academy of Sciences by a geologist who had ridden a mule (!) up the very same route King claimed to be perilous. Embarrassed, King returned to the Sierra in 1873 to climb the real Whitney summit. But his earlier mistake and hyperbole were to haunt him the rest of his life. In an 1874 edition of *Mountaineering,* King acknowledged his error, then subsequently refused to allow any more editions of the book to be published, buying up the book plates and locking them in his closet.

In the following letter, Muir's advice that "travelers who dislike climbing" take the southern route (King's route), and his statement that Mount Langley might "easily be ascended to the very summit on horseback" may well have infuriated the already embarrassed King. Some years later King was to call Muir a geological "amateur" whose

theories of glaciology led only to "hopeless floundering."[1] Muir later
suggested that "well-seasoned limbs" would enjoy climbing Whitney
via his eastern and direct route, while "soft, succulent people should
go the mule way."

Ascent of Mount Whitney

Men ascend mountains as instinctively as squirrels ascend
trees, and, of course, the climbing of Mount Whitney was a
capital indulgence, apart from the enjoyment drawn from landscapes and scientific pursuits.[2] We set out from the little village
of Independence with plenty of excelsior determination, Bayley,
as usual, rejoicing in warwhoops, much to the wonderment of
sober passers-by. The massive sun-beaten Sierra rose before us
out of the gray sagebrush levels like one vast wall 9,000 feet
high, adorned along the top with a multitude of peaks that seem
to have been nicked out in all kinds of fanciful forms for the
sake of beauty. Mount Whitney is one of those wall-top peaks,
having no special geological significance beyond the scores of
nameless peaks amid which it stands, and possessing so little
appreciable individuality that we did not meet a single person
living here who was able to point it out. Where is Mount Whitney? we would ask the teamsters and farmers we met between
Independence and Lone Pine.[3] "Don't know exactly," was the
common reply. "One of them topmost peaks you see yonder,"

1. Clarence King, ed., *Systematic Geology: Report of the Fortieth Parallel
Survey* (Washington: Government Printing Office, 1878), p. 478.
2. Mount Whitney, elevation 14,449', is today usually climbed by the gradually ascending trail from Whitney Portal to Trial Crest, then along the ridge
near Mount Muir to the summit. Muir was the first to climb the mountain from
the east, and his route, which lay generally to the north of the present trail, followed the North Fork of Lone Pine Creek past Clyde Meadow and over to
Iceberg Lake, where a climb was made of the Sierra crest, probably just south of
Mount Russell. The final leg of his ascents varied, as he explains in this letter.
3. Independence, formerly Fort Independence, lies at the eastern base of the
Sierra about ten miles below Kearsarge Pass; some twenty miles south is the town
of Lone Pine, from where it is possible to see Mount Whitney.

at the same time waving their hands indefinitely toward the wilderness of summits.

For those travelers who dislike climbing, the proper way to the top of Whitney lies from Lone Pine around the southern extremity of the high Sierra to the Upper Kern river Valley, by way of Cottonwood Creek. The mountain is thus approached from the west where the slopes are lowest, and where one may easily ride to an elevation of 12,000 feet above sea-level, leaving only a light foot scramble of between 2,500 and 3,000 feet to be made in reaching the utmost summit; whereas, by the quick direct route discovered by me two years ago, leading up the east flank of the range opposite Lone Pine, the elevation to be overcome by foot climbing amounts to about 9,000 feet.

THE ASCENT

With the exception of our one young student, our party were mountaineers, and we chose the eastern route, the mountain influences bearing us buoyantly aloft without leaving us any gross weight to overcome by ordinary conscious effort. On the first day we rode our mules some eighteen miles, through a fine, evenly-planted growth of sage-brush to the foot of the range, immediately west of Lone Pine. Here we "found *a man*," a whole-souled Welchman [*sic*], by the name of Thomas, with whom we camped for the night, and where all was made ready for an early start up the mountain next morning. Each carried a loaf of bread, a handful of tea and a tincup, and a block of beef about four inches in diameter, cut from the lean heartwood of a steer; the whole compactly bundled in half a blanket, and carried by a strap passed over the shoulder, and beside these common necessaries, Bayley carried a small bottle of spirits for healing, sustaining, and fortifying uses, in case of encounters with triangular headed snakes, bears, Indians, mountain rams, noxious night airs, snow storms, etc.; and in case of vertigo and difficult breathing at great heights, together with broken bones, flesh wounds, skin erosions, abrasions, contusions. For in prudence, is it not well to realize that "something might happen," and well to have a helpful spirit—a guardian angel in a bottle ever near?

The highway by which we ascended was constructed by an ancient glacier that drew its sources from the eastern flank of Mount Whitney and the adjacent summits, and poured its icy floods into Owens Valley, which during the glacial epoch was a sea of ice.[4] Of this mighty, rock-crushing ice-river, scarce a vestige remains, and its channel is now occupied by a dashing crystal stream that kept us good company all the way to the summit. The day was warm, and many were the delicious lavings we enjoyed among its pools beneath the cooling shadows of its leafy border groves. The great declivity of the cañon gives rise to numerous rapids and cascades, along the edges of which, soil of sufficient depth for the best wild gardens and thickets cannot be made to lie; but small oval flats of rich alluvium occur between the rocky inclines, rising one above another in almost regular order like stairs. Here the alder and the birch grow close together in luxuriant masses, crossing their topmost branches above the streams, and weaving a bowery roof.[5]

A MINOR YOSEMITE

At an elevation of about 8,000 feet above the sea we come to a fine Yosemite Valley, where a large tributary glacier from the southwest had united with the main trunk. The sheer granite walls rise loftily into the pure azure to the height of from two to three thousand feet, sculptured in true Yosemitic style, and pre-

4. Recent geological theories place the Ice Epochs before the upheavals which lifted the Sierra's eastern flank, and therefore give more emphasis than did Muir to water erosion as the chief cause of the escarpment valleys; moreover, the great height of the Sierra crest above the Owens Valley floor was due to down-faulting, or sinking, of the Owens region, of a type Muir did not believe was possible ("God never made the bottom drop out of anything," he once said in countering Whitney's explanation of Yosemite Valley's creation). For a discussion of Sierra geology, see François E. Matthes, *The Incomparable Valley: A Geologic Interpretation of the Yosemite,* ed. Fritiof Fryxell (Berkeley and Los Angeles: University of California Press, 1950). The Muir-Whitney dispute is discussed by John Robinson in "The Creation of Yosemite Valley: A Scientific Controversy from the Nineteenth Century," *Pacific Historian* 24:4 (Winter 1980): 377–85.

5. The white alder (*Alnus rhombifola*) and mountain alder (*A. tenuifola*) are most commonly found along streams below 7000'; the water birch (*Betula ocidentalis*) is the most common tree along streams of this portion of the eastern Sierra escarpment.

senting a most lavish abundance of spires and gothic gables along the top, with huge buttresses and free and interlacing arches down the face, with numerous caves and niches for ornamental groups of pines. Nor is there any lack of white falling water, nor of tender joyous plant beauty, to complement every manifestation of stern, enduring rockiness. For a distance of two or three miles above the head of this wild Yosemite the ascent is rather steep and difficult, because the canyon walls come sheer down in many places to the brink of the rushing stream, leaving no free margin for a walk, and in many places a dense growth of alder and willow, crushed and felted with the pressure of winter snow, renders the gorge all but impassable, the dead limbs all sloping downward, meeting the up-struggling mountaineer like clusters of presented bayonets.

The difficulties I encountered in forcing my way through this portion of the gorge during my first ascent caused me to scan the gaps and terraces of the south wall, with a view to avoiding the bottom of the gorge altogether. Coming to the conclusion that the thing was at least practicable, I led the party over a rough earthquake talus, beneath an overhanging cliff, and up an extremely steep and narrow gully to the edge of the main canyon wall.

AN ACCIDENT—GLACIER MEADOWS—
A GLIMPSE OF WHITNEY

Here occurred the only accident worth mentioning connected with the trip. Washburn, who climbs slowly, was soon a considerable distance in the rear, and I sat down at the head of the narrow gully to wait for him. Bayley soon came up somewhat breathless with exertion, and without thinking of consequences, loosened a big boulder that went bounding down the narrow lane with terrible energy, followed by a train of small stones and dust. Washburn was about a hundred feet below, and his destruction seemed inevitable, as he was hemmed in between two sheer walls not five feet apart. We shouted to give him warning, and listened breathlessly until his answering shout assured us of his escape. On coming up weary and nerve-shaken with fright, he reported that the dangerous mass shot immediately over him as he lay crouched in a slight hollow. Falling rocks, single or in avalanches, form the greatest of all the perils that beset the mountaineer among the summit peaks.

By noon we reached a genuine glacier meadow, where we disturbed a band of wild sheep that went bounding across the stream and up the precipitous rocks out of sight. We were now 10,000 feet above sea level, and were in the Alps; having passed in half a day from the torrid plains of Owens Valley to an Arctic climate, cool and distant in all its sounds and aspects as Greenland or Labrador.

Here we caught our first fair view of the jagged, storm-worn crest of Mount Whitney, yet far above and beyond, looming gray and ruin-like from a multitude of shattered ridges and spires. Onward we pushed, unwearied, waking hosts of new echoes with shouts of emphatic excelsior. Along the green, plushy meadow, following its graceful margin curves, then up rugged slopes of gray bowlders that had thundered from the shattered heights in an earthquake, then over smooth polished glacier pavements to the utmost limits of the timber line, and our first day's climbing was done.

CAMPING ON THE MOUNTAIN

Our elevation was now eleven thousand five hundred feet, and as the afternoon was less than half done, we had ample time to prepare beds, make tea, and gather a store of pitchy pine roots for our night fire. We chose the same camping ground I had selected two years before on the edge of a sedgy meadow enamelled with buttercups and daisies, near a waterfall and snowbank, and surrounded with ranks of majestic alps. There were the withered pine tassels on which I had slept, and circling heap of stones built as a shelter from the down rushing night wind, and the remains of my wood-pile gathered in case of a sudden snow-storm. Each made his own tin cupful of tea, and dinner was speedily accomplished. Then bed-building was vigorously carried on, each selecting willow shoots, pine tassels or withered grass with a zeal and naturalness whose sources must lie somewhere among our ancient grandfathers, when "wild in woods," etc. I have experimented with all kinds of plant pillows with especial reference to softness and fragrance, and here I was so happy as to to invent a new one, composed of the leaves and flowers of the alpine dodecatheon,[6] elastic, fragrant and truly beautiful. Here we rested as only mountaineers can. The wind fell to soft whispers, keen spiky shadows stole over the meadow, and pale rosy light bathed the savage peaks, making a picture of Nature's repose that no words can ever describe. Darkness came, and the night wind began to flow like a deep and gentle river; the cascades nearby sounded all its note with most impressive distinctness, and the sky glowed with living stars. Then came the moon, awakening the giant peaks that seemed to return her solemn gaze. The grand beauty of our chamber walls came out in wonderfully clear relief, white light and jet shadows revealing their wild fountain architecture divested of all distracting details.

STILL UPWARD—GLACIER LAKES—VEGETATION

We rose early and were off in the first flush of dawn, passing first over a rounded ice-polished brow, then along the north shore of a glacier lake whose simple new-born beauty enchanted us all. It lay imbedded in the rocks like a dark blue green—a perfect mountain eye. Along its northern shore we sped joyously, inspired with the fresh unfolding beauties of the morning, leaping huge blocks of porphyry laid down by an ancient earthquake, and over morainal embankments and slopes of crystalline gravel; every muscle in harmonious accord, thrilled and toned and yielding us the very highest pleasures of the flesh. Speedily we meet the glances of another crystal lake, and of our dearest alpine flowers; azure daisies and primulas, cassiope and bryanthus,[7] the very angels of mountain flora. Now the sun

6. Any of the species of "shooting stars." Muir was indulging himself with a pillow made of the alpine species *Dodecatheon alpinum*.

7. These typically Sierra high country flowers are: "Cut-leaved Daisy" (*Erigeron compositus*); "rock fringe" (*Epilobium obcordatum*), of the evening primrose family; "white heather" (*Cassiope mertensina*); and "red heather" (*Phyllodoce breweri*.)

rose, and filled the rocks with beamless spiritual light. The Clark crow was on the wing, and the frisky tamias and marmot[8] came out to bask on favorite boulders, and the daisies spread their rays and were glad. Above the second lake basin we found a long up-curving field of frozen snow, across which we scampered, with our breasts filled with exhilarating azure, leaping with excess of strength and rolling over and over on the clean snow-ground like dogs.

SCALING THE DIVIDING RIDGE—AT THE SUMMIT

We followed the snow nearly to its upper limit, where it leaned against the dividing axis of the range, placing our feet in hollows melted by radiated heat from stones shot down from the crumbling heights. To scale the dividing ridge in front was impossible, for it swept aloft in one colossal wave with a vertical shattered crest. We were therefore compelled to swerve to the north; then carefully picking our way from ledge to ledge, gained the summit about 8 A.M. There stood Mount Whitney now without a single ridge between; its spreading base within a stone's throw; its pointed, helmet-shaped summit 2,000 feet above us. We gazed but a moment on the surrounding grandeur: the mighty granite battlements; the dark pine woods far below, and the glistening streams and lakes; then dashed adown the western slope into the valley of the Kern. On my first ascent I pushed direct to the summit up the north flank, but the memories of steep slopes of ice and snow over which I had to pick my way, holding on by small points of stones frozen more or less surely into the surface, where a single slip would result in death, made me determine that no one would ever be led by me through the same dangers. I therefore led around the north base of the mountain to the westward, much to Bayley's disgust, who declared that he could, or at least *would* follow wherever I was able to lead. Cautious Washburn wisely gave in his adhesion for the longer and safer route, and I remained firm in avoiding the dangerous ice slopes. We passed along the rocky shores of a lake

8. The shy "yellow-bellied marmot" (*Marmota flaviventris*) is common among the rock and talus slopes of the alpine region.

whose surface was still (July 21st) covered with cakes of winter ice, around the edges of which the color of the water was a beautiful emerald green. Beyond the lake we gradually climbed higher, mounting in a spiral around the northwest shoulder of the mountain, crossing many a strong projecting buttress and fluting hollow, then bearing to the left urged our way directly to the summit. Higher, higher, we climbed with muscles in excellent poise, the landscape becoming more and more glorious as the wild Alps rose in the tranquil sky. Bayley followed closely, lamenting the absence of danger, whenever in this attenuated air he could command sufficient breath. Washburn seldom ventured to leap from rock to rock, but moved mostly on all fours, hugging projecting angles and boulders in a sprawled, outspread fashion, like a child clinging timidly to its mother, often calling for directions around this or that precipice, and careful never to look down for fear of giddiness, yet from first to last evincing a most admirable determination and persistence of the slow and sure kind. Shortly after 10 o'clock A.M. we gained the utmost summit—a fact duly announced by Bayley as soon as he was rested into a whooping condition, and before any note was taken of the wilderness of landscapes by which we were zoned. Undemonstrative Washburn examined the records of antecedent visitors, then remarked with becoming satisfaction, "I'm the first and only student visitor to this highest land in North America."

SUCCESSIVE ASCENTS—CLARENCE KING'S MISTAKE

This mountain was first ascended in the summer of 1873, by a party of farmers and stock raisers from Owens Valley, who were taking exercise. It was ascended a few weeks later by Clarence King, myself and a few others, and this summer by one party besides our own.

The first climbers of the mountain named it Fisherman's Peak. The mountain climbed by Clarence King several years previous, and supposed by him to be the highest in the range, and on which he then bestowed the name of Whitney, lies some six or seven miles to the south of the present Mount Whitney, alias

Fisherman's Peak.[9] The old Mount Whitney, though upward of 14,000 feet in height, may easily be ascended to the very summit on horseback, and, in general, every mountain in the range may easily be ascended by climbers of ordinary nerve and skill. Mount Whitney has not yet been accurately measured, although fair approximations have been reached, making its height about 14,800 feet above the sea. Mount Shasta, situated near the northern extremity of the range, is a few hundred feet lower; yet its individual height, measured from its own proper base, is from nine to eleven thousand feet, while that of Whitney is only from two to three thousand. The former is a colossal cone rising in solitary grandeur and might well be regarded as an object of religious worship; the latter is one of many peaks of an irregular and fragmentary form. Shasta was built *upward* by fire, Whitney was built *downward* by ice. I would gladly try to write a few words concerning the landscapes that lay manifest in all their glory beneath and around us, but there is no room here. We left the summit about noon and swooped to the torrid plains before sundown, as if dropping out of the sky.

INDEPENDENCE,
AUGUST 17, 1875

9. Actually, King correctly identified the Whitney peak as the nation's tallest when first seeing it from Mount Brewer in the summer of 1864. See the chapter entitled "Mount Whitney" in King, *Mountaineering in the Sierra Nevada;* and Farquhar, *History of the Sierra Nevada,* pp. 173–87, as well as Farquhar's account of King's mountaineering in the same volume, pp. 145–54.

Muir concluded his excursion into the southern Sierra by returning to Yosemite via the eastern base of the Sierra, traveling north from the little town of Independence to Mono Lake. Muir found the entire route to be a grand geological laboratory of volcanic cones and glacial pathways, and the following *Bulletin* article explains the part both played in shaping the region's topography.

Muir did not believe in the "down-faulting" theory which now is used to explain the great Sierra escarpment, continuing instead to hold to the single Ice Age hypothesis; yet his descriptions of the eastern Sierra were largely geologically correct, and moreover (and more important), they were the first detailed descriptions of Owens Valley and Mono Basin to appear in print.

The entire Sierra escarpment held his attention, but it was the stark beauty of Mono Lake which seems most to have captured his imagination. The appeal in the article's conclusion—for Californians to look to their own state for their tourism—suggests Muir knew the abuses he had witnessed in Yosemite and the southern portion of the Sierra would soon occur elsewhere in the mountains. Muir's concerns were rapidly drawing together his science and his ethics.

From Fort Independence

In every country the mountains are fountains, not only of rivers but of men. Therefore we all are born mountaineers, the offspring of rock and sunshine; and, although according to ordinary commercial methods of computation it may seem a long way down through lichen and pinetree to God-like human beings, yet measured by other standards the distance becomes scarcely appreciable.

FORT INDEPENDENCE

In a few hours after leaving the summit of Mount Whitney we[1] found ourselves in the middle of a cluster of beautiful

1. Muir's companions continued to be Bayley, Washburn, and perhaps "Buckskin Bill."

homes, where, instead of the company of marmots and mountain sheep, we enjoyed the rare luxury of meeting cultured men
and women, living bravely and beautifully in an oasis of flowery
verdure out in the gray hot sage plains of Owens Valley. This
was at Fort Independence,[2] three miles north of the village of
that name. The old adobe buildings of the past were cast down
during the memorable earthquake of March 26, 1872,[3] and have
been replaced by wooden structures, with a view to future
shocks in this volcanic region. The buildings occupied by the
officers, besides being commodious and substantial, show rare
taste in their proportions and finish, the redwood and pine of
which they are built having their contrasting colors and their
grain beautifully brought out in the paneled walls. We arrived
here on one of the best of those lovely purple afternoons for
which the dry desert regions lying to the east of the Sierra are
remarkable. Ice-cooled breezes from the mountains oozed softly
through an embankment of shade trees, flooding the halls and
verandahs with delicious tempered air. Roses bloomed profusely
around the walls, and numerous flute-voiced streamlets flowed
through gardens filled with showy exotics, and fields of blue
alfalfa all in bloom, producing dreamy Oriental impressions, as
if one were seated in a Damascus rose garden reading *Arabian
Nights*. Such are the homes to which a bevy of refined ladies and
gentlemen bade us welcome on descending from the icy recesses
of the Sierra, notwithstanding our bandit clothing and accoutre-
ments. Our clothing was by this time considerably corroded and
covered with strange camp stains, colored like Alpine lichens,
and with here and there a patch of gum and rosin in which were
imbedded samples of every rock and soil from all the various
geological regions we had visited.

OWENS VALLEY—LAVA FLOOD

Gladly we would have lingered, but our work drove us on, and
the next sunrise saw us tracing a dusty track through the gray

2. Now Old Fort Independence.
3. For Muir's reaction to the earthquake at the time it occurred, see Badè,
Life and Letters, 1:326–28. The tremendous quake was associated with a shifting
of the Sierra fault and caused severe damage to the small towns lying at the
eastern base of the Sierra Nevada; graves of several victims may still be found in
the town of Lone Pine, California.

levels of Owens Valley. Onward we rode northward along the base of the range, which for many a mile, as far as the eye could reach, stretched unbrokenly like a wall, topped with towers and giant castles. A few miles ahead we observe a weird black flood of lava interrupting the sober gray of the plain, and so fresh-looking and unaltered that it seems to be flowing, and we easily traced it to its source, in a smoothly tapered volcano, up against the granite bosses of the mountains. Soon we approach the outermost of its strange currents, and make our way over their flinty frozen surfaces, marking where the rocky flood flowed deepest, when it was a glowing molten mass, and where, in cooling, its contractions threw it into jagged folds and hillocks. We see hollows and chasms filled with cinders and scoriae, the entire surface being wholly unchanged, save where an ancient water flood from the canyon heaped gravel along its sides. Crossing this strange fire-field we again find ourselves on the gray sandy levels, but speedily come upon another stream of frozen lava, black and vesicular like the first, and post-glacial in age, having been outpoured at a comparatively recent date, since the Sierra received its present conformation.⁴ Beyond in this mysterious land of fire we behold yet another lava-flood curving down into the plain, but this time from the east, the volcanoes from which it poured being conspicuously located on the lower slopes of the Inyo range.

At Bishop's Creek, we come upon a fine fertile sheet of al-luvium deposited by the mountain streams in a glacier lake basin, now dotted with houses and fields of hay and wheat. Holding our way still northward, we reach a wall of basaltic bluffs stretching entirely across the head of Owens Valley from the Sierra to the Inyo range. This is the eroded edge of a massive tableland of rose-colored lava, dividing the Mono and Owens River basins; and as we traverse its canyons and gorges, and note how its surface is strewn with slate and granite bowlders from the Sierra and grooved with glacier canyons, we learn that this

4. Muir did not know that the Sierra escarpment was formed more by the down-faulting of the Owens Valley than by the uplifting of the mountains. He is right, however, in dating the volcanic activity he was here exploring after the major ice periods. The area Muir describes is the Lava Creek and Crater Mountain region near Big Pine, California.

lava is far more ancient—that it is pre-glacial in age, and flowed from volcanoes not now visible, perhaps destroyed during the glacial epoch.[5]

A PLEASANT CHANGE—LONG VALLEY

Winding through the rocky defiles and waterless hollows of this ancient lava field we suddenly emerge upon the green, boggy flats of Long Valley, dotted with thousands of horned cattle and veined with mazy streams shining in the sun like strips of silver. The valley is about twelve miles long and lies at an elevation of 7,500 feet above the sea, and forms one of the most important summer pastures of this remarkable region. Along the northern margin of the valley we find the volcanic forces still active and manifested in numerous hot springs, geysers and solfataras,[6] ranged around the base of lava bluffs that bound the valley on the north. Here, too, the wild landscapes are indescribably sublime. The Sierra on the left, Inyo Mountains on the right, a purple table-land between, with lofty volcanic cones rising beyond, colored red and blue and ashy gray, and in the foreground the green meadow, level as a lake.[7]

Yonder looms the commanding form of Mount Ritter the noblest mountain of the range, standing King in the heart of the California Alps, the Switzerland of the Sierra. Riding around this splendid mountain lawn we pass many a granite buttress, that come plunging down abruptly and plant their feet in the valley level, like headlands standing out into the sea, and many a bright-dashing stream-feeder of Owens river, the longest tributary of which has its sources in the glaciers of Ritter and the Minarets.

5. During the four distinct ice ages of the Pleistocene Epoch there occurred strong faulting movements along this part of the eastern Sierra. The country to the east of the fault sank, the great escarpment was formed, and in the southern and middle parts of the range local lava flows filled the valleys and flowed out into the Owens plain.

6. These vents are still active. Indeed, the entire region around Mammoth Lakes is considered by geologists to be an active volcanic site.

7. This region is now inundated by the water of Crowley Lake, a part of the City of Los Angeles water system.

MONO VALLEY—DEAD LAKES

Crossing over to Mono, we ride along the bottom and around the shores of many a dead lake, now made into gardens, and filled with delicate wild flowers. The yellow pine is planted over all this streamless wilderness, maintaining a vigorous growth, and ripening its large purple cones upon dry lava rocks, seemingly as much at home as when growing with the sugar pine on rich and well watered moraines. Here we noticed thousands of trees that were encircled with shallow trenches dug by the Pah Ute Indians, for the capture of large green worms, the larvae of a species of silk worm which they use as food.[8]

MORE VOLCANOES

Just before descending into the Mono basin we come upon a magnificent cluster of volcanoes, so perfect in form and fresh-looking we half expect to see fire rushing from their rounded craters. The loftiest of the group rises about 2,700 feet above the level of Mono Lake.[9] They are all post-glacial, having been erupted from what was once the bottom of the south end of Mono Lake through stratified glacial drift, and have scattered during their numerous periods of activity showers of ashes and cinders over all the adjacent glacier canyons and mountain-tops within a radius of twenty or thirty miles.

To the westward of the cones fine sections occur in the ancient lavas belonging to the tableland extending to Owens Valley, wherein the trap formation is beautifully developed.

8. There were perhaps 2,000 Eastern and Western Mono (Paiute) Indians living in Muir's day. They were frequent users of the trail systems across the Sierra and traded with the Miwoks of Yosemite, exchanging for acorns the nut of the singleleaf pinyon pine and the larvae of the "koo-chah-bee" fly (*Ephydra hians*). William Brewer noted that "hundreds of bushels [of the larvae] could be collected. . . . The Indians come far and near to gather them. The Indians gave me some; it does not taste bad, and if one were ignorant of its origin, it would make a fine soup." (Brewer, *Up and Down California*, p. 417.) The "species of silk worm" Muir mentions is probably a tent caterpillar (family *Laciocampidae*), so-called for the protective silk-like web it spins on trees. The local Indians' diet of larvae resulted in their name "fly people," or "Monos." See Verna R. Johnson, *Sierra Nevada* (Boston: Houghton Mifflin, 1970), pp. 201–3.

9. The Mono Craters. The highest is Crater Mountain, at 9,172 feet.

"View of the Mono Plain from the Foot of Bloody Cañon." Engraving by E. Heineman. In Muir, *The Mountains of California*, p. 97.

MONO LAKE—A LOVELY SCENE

Coming out in full view of the Lake, the landscape becomes exquisitely beautiful, notwithstanding the general impression of arid barrenness. The Lake, though bitter as the Dead Sea, is yet translucent as Tahoe, and in calms mirrors the colors of its shores and the massive cumuli that pile themselves in the purple sky above it as no fresh water lake ever can. And the Mono Desert is a desert of flowers the beauty of which the most loving pen will never describe.

ANTAGONISTIC FORCES OF FIRE AND ICE

Nowhere within the bounds of our wonder-filled land are the antagonistic forces of fire and ice brought so closely and contrastingly together. The volcanic phenomena are so striking we seem to be among the very hearths and firesides of nature, yet standing amid drifting ashes, and turning to the mountains we behold huge moraines sweeping from the shadowy jaws of cañons out into the basin, marking the pathways of scores of glaciers that crawled down the mountain sides and through their icy snouts laden with *debris* out into the lake, as they are now descending into the Greenland seas. Bergs were formed here also, floating in grinding drifts, and not a single Arctic character was wanting where now the traveler is scorched and blinded in a glare of tropic light. But nature never halts. Climates change and run through their courses in appointed times like organized beings; the snow-flowers fall less lavishly from the mountain clouds; the glaciers melt in the warmer sunbeams and slowly withdraw into their upper strongholds of shade. The lake has now a free shore, and plants flocks to the genial soil. The summers still growing warmer, one by one the glaciers die; fewer streams descend into the waning lake, until evaporation equals the inflowing water and it becomes the acrid dead sea of to-day. The terraces around the lake record the fact that some time subsequent to the close of the glacial period the water stood 650 feet higher than the present level, and these successive changes of level are so related to the withdrawal of the glaciers that flowed into the basin as to constitute cause and effect.

BLOODY CANYON—MONO JOE

Joe Boler's ranch, at the foot of Bloody Canyon, is the camping centre for all the Mono excursionists from Yosemite, the only habitation for many miles. Mono Joe is a man worth knowing. He came here four years ago, weighing nothing in the gold scales, but possessed of plenty of Teutonic pluck and energy. He found here a stream and a patch of sage plain, and bringing the two together the irrigation caused the desert to blossom as the hay field. He took stock on shares (not mining stock), made butter, raised calves and colts, drank nothing stronger than milk or Bloody Canyon water, and is now worth in the gold market $30,000. Here is an example for tradeless young men and complaining Micawbers, so abundant in our streets.

BACK TO YOSEMITE—A WORD TO CALIFORNIANS

From here we return to Yosemite by the old glacial pathway of Bloody Canyon,[10] thus completing one of the most perfect mountain excursions that may be made.

Californians are little aware of the grandeur of their own land, as is manifested by their leaving it for foreign excursions whenever they become able—leaving the wonders of our unrivalled plains and mountains wholly unrecognized. One mile traveled in a vertical direction is equivalent to a thousand in the direction of the poles. We have Laplands and Labradors of our own, and alps rivaling all that Switzerland can boast, and streams from glacier-caves, rivers of mercy sacred as the Himalaya-born Ganges. We have our Shasta Vesuvius also,[11] and Bay of Naples, and over here among our inland plains are African Saharas, Death Valleys and deserts, with sand storms and green oases where congregate the travelers, coming in long caravans, the trader with his gold and the Pah Ute Indian with his weapons— the Bedouin of the California deserts.

YOSEMITE VALLEY,
SEPTEMBER 1875

10. This seldom-used trail (about five miles south of present-day Highway 120) extends from Walker Lake to Yosemite's Mono Pass. Brewer used it in 1863 and noted how apt was the name of the trail: his horses were so cut by the sharp rocks that the trail was "literally sprinkled with blood from the animals."
11. The famous Vesuvius had erupted in 1872.

PART FOUR
Return to the Sequoia Groves

> How much further the Sequoia belt
> extends in this direction, is a question
> I hope to settle some time before the
> coming on of winter storms. . . . I
> will make a way, and love of King
> Sequoia will make all the labor light.
>
> October 1875

Sequoiadendron giganteum—the Big Trees—had fascinated Muir
from the moment he first saw them. Their girth and imposing stature
were a source of constant wonderment, and for Muir they served as a
sort of botanical guidepost pointing towards the possibilities of life.
"I'm in the woods, woods, woods, and they are in *me-ee-ee*," he had
once written to Mrs. Carr; ". . . The King tree and I have sworn
eternal love—sworn it without swearing, and I've taken Sacrament
with Douglas squirrel, drunk Sequoia wine, Sequoia blood, and with
its rosy purple drops I am writing this woody gospel letter."[1]

To better know this tree, Muir set out from Yosemite on one last
mountain journey of the 1875 season. He would travel alone, walking
nearly 600 miles, accompanied only by a mule named "Brownie."
His goal was to seek out every Sequoia forest between the Yosemite's
Mariposa Grove and the Kaweah River region lying some two hundred miles to the south. As had become his habit, he recorded his
findings in notebooks, and he managed to send at least five letters to
the *Bulletin.* Four reached the newspaper and are reprinted in the
final part of this book.

Muir first explored the Big Tree grove lying some twenty miles
south of Wawona, and wrote of his discoveries in the article entitled
"The Fresno Grove of Sequoia." This letter, among the most charming of his descriptive writings from the time, includes the account of
his accidental encounter with a hermit named John Nelder. Muir

1. Badè, *Life and Letters,* 1:271.

"Hercules." Pencil drawing of a fallen sequoia by Edward Visher, ca. 1880. Courtesy the Bancroft Library.

contrasts the calm life of his new-found friend with the hard and
degrading one Nelder had lived as a miner during the Gold Rush. "It
is delightful," Muir noted, "to see how sensitively he feels the silent
influences of the woods."

During this one trip Muir would visit fully two-thirds of the
seventy-five sequoia groves of the Sierra Nevada. He explored them
by daylight and once, during a forest fire, by firelight. The trip was
hard, and he was alternately hungry and exhausted; yet, he insisted,
he would ". . . make a way, and love of King Sequoia will make all
the labor light." Muir clearly prized this trip into the groves, perhaps
sensing it would be the last major journey he would make in solitude.
His later explorations in Nevada and the Northwest would be
deliberately planned and executed, and would culminate in the
Glacier Bay "expeditions" of the 1880s. The inevitable result of those
trips would be fame and the subsequent loss of privacy. That, and his
marriage, would take from him the luxury of untimed explorations.
Thus this second trip of 1875 was to be his final banquet of discovery, closing in a real way the "Merced and Tuolumne chapter" of
his life when his discoveries were made "free from time and wheels."
He would cherish the memories of this trip for a lifetime, and
portions of these *Bulletin* articles were to turn up later in his future
articles and books, though not with the same freshness as here.
Seldom again would Muir be alone in the wilderness, and never again
would he be there in the same measureless way.

The Royal Sequoia

A few day ago while camped in the fir woods on the head of
one of the southmost tributaries of the Merced, I caught sight of
a lofty granite dome, called Wa-mello by the Indians,[2] looming
into the free sky far above the forest, and though now studying
trees, I soon found myself upon its commanding summit. Here I
obtained glorious views of the wide fertile valleys of the Fresno
[River], filled with forests; innumerable spires of yellow pines
towering above one another on the sloping heights; miles of

2. This is the Fresno Dome, located some fifty miles south of Yosemite Valley.

sugar-pine with feathery arms outstretched in the sunshine; and toward the southwest I beheld the lofty dome-like crowns of the sequoia, rising here and there out of the green slopes and levels of the pines, singly or densed together in imposing congregations. There is something wonderfully impressive in this tree, even when beheld from a great distance; their dense foliage and smoothly rounded outlines enables one to recognize them at once in any company, to say nothing of their superior size and kingliness. They grow upon ridge tops as well as in sheltered ravines, and when one of the oldest kings attains full stature on some commanding height, he seems the very god of the woods. No tree in the Sierra forest has foliage so densely massed, or presents outlines so constant in form or so finely drawn as Sequoia. Fortunate old trees that have reached their three thousandth birthday without injury from fire or frost, present a mound like summit of warm yellow green foliage. Younger trees are darker in color, and shoot up with summits comparatively sharp, but not at all arrowy like those of the fir or pine. Their colossal brown trunks finely tapered and furrowed, may often be seen glowing in the sun, branchless, to a height of 150 feet, yet not altogether leafless, for green sprays occur at intervals, making flecks of shadow, and seeming to have been pinned on as ornamental rosettes for the sake of beauty alone. The ripe cones are green as cucumbers, and measure about two inches in length and one and a half in diameter, made up of about forty diamond-shaped scales, densely packed with from five to eight seeds at the base of each. Each cone, therefore, contains from two to three hundred seeds. The seeds resemble those of the common parsnips, and are about one-fourth of an inch long by three-sixteenths of an inch wide, the greater portion of the bulk being taken up by a thin, flat, scale-like wing, which, when the seed is set free to seek its fortune, makes it fly off glancingly to its growing place like a boy's kite. The seeds are nearly ripe now, and there is sufficient in this grove alone to plant the globe. No other California conifer produces anything like as many seeds. Some trees certainly ripen more than a million, while one might easily number the nuts of the most fruitful pine in a single day.

COLORING MATTER—TIMBER OF THE BIG TREE

At the base of the scales and in contact with the seeds there is a considerable quantity of a dark, gritty substance, which dissolves readily in water and yields a magnificent purple color which may probably be utilized; certainly it seems well worthy of careful experiment, as it may be obtained in large quantities at a very slight cost, and the quantity of coloring matter, to say nothing of other properties, must make it exceedingly valuable should it prove available. A single cone will color a bucket of water a delicious transparent purple, that seems perfectly constant. I have myself used it as ink, and I find it first-rate; and I have also drank it, hoping thereby to improve my color and render myself more tree-wise and sequoical.[3]

The timber of the Big Tree, besides being beautiful, is easily worked, and is more enduring than any other that I know of. Build a house of sequoia logs and lay the foundation upon solid granite, and that house will last about as long as the rock. Or fell a sequoia in the dank decomposing woods and with it lay any species of oak, pine or fir, and these will be rotted and weathered out of sight before the main body of sequoia will have suffered the slightest appreciable decay or changed color. Indeed, fire seems to be the only decomposing agent that has any effect upon it. I have in my possession a specimen of the wood of the Sierra sequoia, which neither in color, strength or any other property can be distinguished from specimens cut from living trees; yet the trunk from which this specimen was obtained has lain upon the damp ground exposed to all kinds of weathering for at least three hundred and eighty years, and probably twice as long or more. The evidence in the case is simply this: a tree fifteen or twenty feet in diameter fell upon one of these Fresno hillsides, and in falling, the ponderous trunk sunk into the ground, thus making a wide ditch or furrow about five or six feet deep, and in the middle of this ditch, where a portion of the trunk had been removed by fire, I found a silver fir (*Picea*

---

3. Several of the letters Muir wrote using this sequoia ink continue to possess a distinctive purplish tone.

Grandis) growing, that is four feet in diameter and three hundred and eighty years old, demonstrating that the age of my specimen must be this great at least. But in order to arrive at the whole age it would of course be necessary to know how many

"View in the Sierra Forest." Engraving by Butler (?), ca. 1875. In Muir, *The Mountains of California,* p. 141.

years elapsed before the portion of the ditch occupied by this silver fir was laid bare by fire and also how much time passed after the clearing of the ditch ere the seed was planted from which the silver fir sprung. This instance of the durability of sequoia timber is by no means a rare one. Fragments of trunks quite as ancient are to be found all through the grove, showing the same wonderful state of preservation, and manifesting their ages by various phenomena whose interpretation can hardly be missed. With regard to the strength of the timber I can say little, never having made any measured tests, yet it appears to be quite as strong as the best fir. When a large tree falls its branches break like the chalky bones of an old man. The main trunk also breaks straight across several times even where the ground is level. One noble specimen that stood two hundred and seventy-five feet high and measured twenty-two feet in diameter at the base was felled a short distance from here by digging around and cutting the main roots, and in falling, the trunk broke straight across in no less than ten places. Although I have observed several trunks of young trees five or six feet in diameter that were felled on rough ground without breaking at all. I also examined some seasoned saplings from three inches to a foot in thickness and found the wood exceedingly tough and elastic.

A DECAYING SPECIES

The big tree is sometimes regarded as a sort of companionless species whose relations have disappeared and as not properly belonging to the flora of the present geological age. These views, however, are mostly erroneous; for though it is true that as a species this mastodon of the vegetable kingdom has come to its period of decadence, many other species among our mountain flora are in the very same condition. Species develop and die like individuals, animals as well as plants; and man, at once the noblest and most conceited species on the globe, will as surely become extinct as mastodon or sequoia. But unless destroyed by man sequoia is in no immediate danger of extinction; it is perhaps scarcely farther past prime than either of our two silver firs, and judging from present conditions and its history as far as I have been able to read, it will live until A.D. 15,000 at least. The

other day I counted no less than 536 sequoia saplings and
sproutings growing promisingly upon a piece of ground not exceeding two acres, and specimens of every age, from one year to
three or four thousand, occur in this one grove. The causes at
work to effect the extinction of the species are chiefly the decay
of the soil on which they are growing, changes in drainage,
changes in climate, and the invasions of other trees, together
with fire and the ax.[4]

THE DOOM OF THE CONIFERAE

As far as the uses of man are concerned the Sierra crop of
coniferae is ripe, and in all probability will be speedily har-
vested. New lumber companies are coming into existence almost
every year. Mills have just been built here, and a flume which is
to extend down the Fresno [River] to the railroad is being
vigorously pushed toward completion, when the magnificent firs
and pines of the Fresno woods, together with the big trees, will
be unsparingly lumbered and floated to market.

A FOREST HERMIT

A while ago I came drifting through the gorges and woods
from the Mariposa trees, arriving here when the grove was full
of noon sunshine, and in sauntering from tree to tree, making
my way through hazel and dogwood and over huge brown logs, I
came suddenly upon a handsome cottage with quaint, old-fash-
ioned chimney and gables, every way uncommon, and so new
and fresh that it still smelled of balsam and rosin, like a newly
felled tree. Strolling forward, wondering to what my strange discovery would lead, I found an old, gray-haired man, sitting at
the door upon a bark stool, weary-eyed and unspeculative and
seemingly surprised that his fine forest hermitage had been discovered. After drinking at the burn that trickles past the door, I

4. Recent investigations point to the necessity of periodic fires to clear the
underbrush from the sequoia groves, thus enabling the seeds to sprout and young
sequoia saplings to survive. The National Park Service has recently experimented
with man-made fires within several of the sequoia forests. The Fresno Grove
Muir describes in this letter was logged extensively in the 1880s. The surviving
trees are known as the Nelder Grove.

sat down beside him and bit by bit he gave me his history, which, in the main, is only a sad illustration of early California life during the gold period, full of intense experiences, now up in exciting success, now down in crushing reverses, the day of life waning meanwhile far into the afternoon, and long shadows turning to the east; health gone and gold; the game played and lost; and now, creeping into this solitude, where he may at least maintain independence, he awaits the coming of night. How sad the tones of the invisible undercurrent of many a life here, now the clang and excitements of the gold battles are over. What wrecks of hopes and health, and how truly interesting are those wrecks. Perhaps no other country in the world contains so many rare and interesting men. The name of my hermit friend is John A. Nelder, a man of broad sympathies, and a keen intuitive observer of nature. Birds, squirrels, plants all receive loving attention, and it is delightful to see how sensitively he feels the silent influences of the woods. How his eye brightens as he gazes upon the grand sequoia kings that stand guard around his cabin. How he pets and feeds the wild quails and Douglass Squirrels, and how tenderly he strokes the sapling sequoias, hoping that they will yet reach the full stature of their race and rule the woods.

To-morrow I will push on southward along the sequoia belt, making special studies of the species and visiting every grove as far as its southernmost limits.

FRESNO GROVE OF BIG TREES,
SEPTEMBER 1875

Muir left the Fresno Grove to continue his investigations of the range's sequoia forests, and for two weeks he pushed southward towards the Kings Canyon and Kaweah regions. Along the way he found many places where the sequoias might have been growing but, to his surprise, discovered no Big Trees until reaching the little forest now known as the McKinley Grove of Sierra Redwoods. From here Muir continued and, according to a later account, it was at this time he first saw Tehipite Valley, the isolated "Yosemite" of the Middle Fork Kings River. This trip southward Muir describes in the following article, "The Giant Forest of the Kaweah."

His main objective continued to be the exploration of the Kings and Kaweah sequoia groves. Along the way he met several pioneers of the region and visited Thomas's and Hyde's mills, two early sequoia lumbering operations which by Muir's account were to take over two million feet of lumber during the season. Muir demonstrates little concern about the sawmills, nor does he seem to be particularly upset about the various "stumps" of sequoia trees which even then were abundant; perhaps he believed the mills too small and the trees too big for sequoia to be endangered. Only later, upon reflection, did Muir realize that in this remote section of the Sierra forces were at work ending the reign of his "King Sequoia." When writing of this same trip some thirty years later, Muir would recall that "in this glorious forest the mill was busy, forming a sore, sad center of destruction, though small as yet, so immensely heavy was the growth."[1]

While Muir no doubt was learning much about the extent of the sequoias and seeing firsthand the sorry legacy left by the mills destined to destroy many of them, the article reproduced here nonetheless remains a bright, joyful account of wilderness travel and is a warm invitation for readers to follow him in his discoveries of King Sequoia.

1. John Muir, *Our National Parks* (Boston: Houghton Mifflin, 1901), quoted in Teale, *Wilderness World,* p. 216.

The Giant Forests of the Kaweah

The motto, "Where there isn't a way, make a way," slips lightly over the tongue of teacher or scholar where no way is needed, but to the traveler in these mountain woods it is soon loaded with meaning. There are ways *across* the range, old ways graded by glaciers and followed by men and bears, but not a single way, natural or artificial, has yet been constructed *along* the range; and the traveler who will thus move in a direction at right angles to the course of the ancient ice rivers must make a way across cañons and ridges laid side by side in endless succession, and all roughened with gorges, gulches, landslips, precipices, and stubborn chaparral almost impenetrable to wolves and bears. Such is the region in which I have been making ways during the last month in pursuit of sequoia gigantae. My own ways are easily made, for my mountaineering has heretofore been almost wholly accomplished on foot, carrying a minimum of every necessary, and lying down by any streamside whenever overtaken by weariness and night. But on this occasion I have been prevailed upon to take a tough, brown mule to carry a pair of blankets and saddle-bags, and many a time while the little hybrid was wedged fast in the rocks, or was struggling out of sight in a wilderness of thorny bushes I have wished myself once more wholly free, notwithstanding the hung[ry] days and cold nights that would follow.

MODIFIED OPINIONS

In my last, written from Fresno Grove, I noticed the prevailing notion concerning the rapid decadence of our mammoth tree as a species, and I am now happy to add, that in tracing the belt from north to south, all the phenomenon bearing upon the question that I have thus far observed, goes to show that the dominion of sequoia gigantea as King of the Sierra forests is not yet passing away, nor are the forces that are to effect its extinction at all visible. No tree in the woods seems more firmly established, or more safely settled down in accordance with climate and soil. The farther south I go the thriftier and more numerous they become, and here on the upper waters of the Kaweah, in-

stead of a few isolated groves hidden away among the sugar
pines, they fill the woods, growing on solid ledges, along water-
course, in the deep moist soil of meadows, and upon avalanche
and glacier debris, with a multitude of seedlings and saplings
crowding around the aged and the dying, ready to take their
places.

A LONG TRAMP

Going southward from Fresno [Grove], not a single sequoia is
found until we reach Dinky Creek, a tributary of the North Fork
of King's river. Here is a small grove of about two hundred trees
growing upon coarse flood soil. The largest specimen measures
thirty-two feet in diameter, four feet above the ground. This
little isolated grove was discovered a few years ago by a couple
of bear hunters, but on account of its remoteness from traveled
roads and trails is hardly known.[2] I spent two weeks among the
canyons of the San Joaquin, exploring every forest where the
sequoia was likely to be, without discovering a single specimen,
or any traces of their former existence. This remarkable gap in
the belt is nearly fifty miles wide. Leaving the secluded colony of
Dinky Creek I led my mule down the canyon of the North Fork
of King's river, forded the stream and climbed to the summit of
the dividing ridge between the North and Middle Forks. Here in
pushing my way southward I was compelled to make a descent
of 7,000 feet at a single swoop. Every pine and fir disappeared
from the woods long ere I reached the bottom of the main canyon. Oaks with bark as white as milk cast their shadows on the
sunburned ground, and not a mountain flower was left me for
company. Here I forded the main river about ten miles below the
King's river, Yosemite, and gladly climbed again to the cool,
pure pine woods.[3]

2. Dinkey Creek is located some fifty miles southeast of Wawona. Muir was
the first to write of this little grove, though not the first to know of it. Pioneer
Frank Dusy, a sheepman in this region, annually took his flocks through the area
and into the Tehipite Valley, going as far east as Bishop's Pass. The sequoias
Muir is here describing are now known as the McKinley Grove.

3. Muir was closely following his 1873 route into this same region. His reference to "King's river, Yosemite" was an obvious attempt to compare favorably
this region with that of the more famous Yosemite Valley of the Merced.

FOREST MONARCHS—THE GRANDEST GROVE OF ALL

Next day I found myself in the sequoia groves, in the neighborhood of the old Thomas' Mill Flat,[4] and bearing off northeastward, I discovered a grand forest nearly six miles long by from one to two miles wide, composed almost exclusively of sequoia, in a fine thrifty condition. This is the first block of sequoia I had met that may be fairly called a forest. It is situated on the south side of the Middle and South Forks of King's river at an elevation of from six to seven thousand five hundred feet above the sea. I learn that a considerable portion of this forest is claimed by Charles Converse, who has formed a company to saw it and flume it to market.[5]

Less than a mile from the southern extremity of this forest we enter the so-called King's river Grove which extend[s] southward to the summit of the Kaweah divide.[6] Descending the rugged south slopes of this divide we at once find ourselves in forests that are still more perfectly ruled by King Sequoia. Immediately to the south of Hyde's mill the mountain crest is crowned with a close continuous growth of the finest big trees I had ever seen. Their noble forms [are] exquisitely outlined on the blue sky, while all the slopes leading from the very bottom of the canyon are densely forested with the same exuberant growth. The finely curved, dome-like summits of almost every tree are seen rising regularly above one another in most imposing majesty. Beyond this first Kaweah forest we descend into what is called Redwood Canyon, whose slopes upon both sides are densely timbered with sequoia, while the noble sugar-pine and fir are hushed and hidden as if not one were present. Between Redwood Canyon and the giant forest there are numerous ridges and hollows subordi-

4. The mill lay close to the General Grant Grove in present-day Sequoia National Park. It was in place as early as 1864, when William Brewer noted, "Here there is a steam sawmill, where two or three families live. And let me describe our delightful camp, so refreshing after the monotony, heat, dust, alkali, discomfort, and tedium of the great plain . . ." See Brewer, *Up and Down California,* p. 514.

5. In the region now called Converse Basin, every sequoia was cut down save the famous Boole Tree. It may be seen near General Grant Grove.

6. The "Giant Forest" of sequoias in Sequoia National Park.

nate to the main canyons of the North and Middle Forks, each of which bears a portion of the more or less continuous belt as it stretches indefinitely southward, waving and wrinkling compliantly to the complicated topography of the basin. Beyond this ragged belt, upon the broad divide separating Marble creek from the Middle Fork, we find The Giant Forest[7] extending from the granite headlands, overlooking the hot foot-hills back to within a few miles of cool glacier fountains, a distance of six or seven miles. The width of the forest varies from one to two or three miles, and the height above sea level from 5,000 to nearly 8,000 feet. It was nearly sundown when I entered this glorious mountain wilderness, and I wandered on through the deep shadowy aisles, wholly dissolved in the strange beauty, as if new arrived from the other world. No amount of familiar communion with the small companies of trees that occur in Calaveras and Tuolumne counties can yield anything more than feeble hints of the sublimity of this grand sequoia realm.

CAMPING IN THE GROVE—A BEAUTIFUL SPOT

I chose a camping ground on the edge of a meadow commanding fine views of the trees as they approach the opening. Their long ranks, clearly outlined against the starry sky, was the grandest night scene I ever beheld in the range. A few sugar pines and silver firs occur here and there, but are so hushed and over-shadowed they exert but little influence and seem like slender grasses growing amid stalks of Indian corn.

In the morning, leaving my jaded mule on the meadow, I sauntered free in this solemn wilderness. Go where I would, sequoia ruled supreme. Trees of every age and size covered the craggiest ridges as well as the fertile, deep-soiled slopes, and planted their colossal shafts along every brook and along the margins of spongy bogs and meadows. Never before had I beheld a mountain meadow environed with sequoias. Here were a series of meadows laid transversely upon the very summit of the main divide as if for ornament, every one of which were thus imbedded in the deep mammoth forest, their smooth emerald

7. Muir claimed in *Our National Parks* (1901) to have been the first to use the phrase "Giant Forest."

"View on the Kern River." Engraver unknown. From a painting by Albert Bierstadt, ca. 1868.

bosoms kept bright by a network of rills and by floods of sunshine poured through the lofty forest aisles. Resting awhile on the margin of the most beautiful of these, my eye soon wandered from the colossal trees to the autumn-tinted willows and huckleberry thickets, and I longed to carry away their divine colors in a picture. Keith[8] and his paints came to mind, and I would fain have gone far to fetch him. No forest picture could equal this. There lay the tranquil sheet of meadow, half a mile long, basking in mellow autumn light, its blushy grasses colored brown and yellow and clear emerald green; its smooth surface picturesquely interrupted with patches of vaccinium, colored red and crimson.[9] Around the margin a fringe of orange, willow and azalea, with scarlet patches of cornel;[10] then the incomparable walls of verdure variously shaded and tinted, dark green of the young spiry trees, the brown and yellow shadings of the old, and their majestic cinnamon-colored trunks in long perspective exquisitely wreathed with small green sprays, and many an aged storm-scarred tree with huge angular arms outspread, overgrown with yellow lichen and surrounded with trees of faultless taper, whose smooth domes seemed to want not a single leaf in their wondrous perfection, while every color seemed steadily to increase in beauty beneath the lavish sunbeams, and every tree hushed, as if conscious of the presence of their Maker.

SIZE OF TREES

Although the area covered with the species increases rapidly towards the south, there is no corresponding difference with regard to size. The average size of full-grown specimens wherever I have been is about 20 feet in diameter and 250 feet high. Trees 25 feet in diameter are not rare and a good many approach 300 feet in height. Occasionally one meets a tree 30 feet in diameter, and very rarely one that is still larger. Thus it will appear that, as far as size is concerned, the Calaveras and Mariposa

8. A reference to Muir's friend William Keith.

9. Probably a reference to the Sierra bilberry (*Vaccinium nivictum*), or huckleberry, common along some high country meadows.

10. This would be the creek dogwood (*Cornus stolonifera*), a relative to the tree-like flowering dogwood; its winter foliage is a deep red color.

trees rival those of King's river and the Kaweah, though far behind in other respects. I have heard vague tiding of the *largest tree* in every forest and grove, but have not yet found it; 40 feet seems the favorite diameter, and this size is maintained among hunters and mountaineers with remarkable constancy. Everybody one meets had heard of this tree, and knows *nearly* where it is, but none *exactly*. It is always ahead. At present it is situated, according to the latest accounts, upon a steep declivity on the north side of the South Fork of Tule river. One man has been within a mile of it. Another has seen it, but did not measure it, etc. Fortunately, the mere size of the one biggest of the big is of little consequence. The largest measured by me is a stump 80 or 90 feet high, situated on the south side of the Middle Fork of King's river. At a height of 4 feet above the ground it is 35 feet 8 inches inside the bark, and a plank this wide could be obtained from it of solid wood, without a decayed fibre.

HARD WORK AHEAD

How much further the sequoia belt extends in this direction, is a question I hope to settle some time before the coming on of winter storms; but there is hard mountaineering ahead. Standing here on the cañon-brink of this middle fork of the Kaweah, I see long ranks of rocky headlands stretching far into the smoky distance, and plunging down vaguely into profound cañon depths; but I can climb and cross them all, and ford every river. I will make a way, and love of King Sequoia will make all the labor light.

PLUNO,
OCTOBER 19, 1875

Sometime after writing the previous letter, Muir composed an article
entitled "The Southern Limit of the Sequoia," in which no doubt he
described the conclusion of his trip among the valleys of the Kaweah
River. If mailed to the *Bulletin,* the article was not published. However, the journals from the trip exist, as does a much later account of
the travels which Muir included in *Our National Parks* (1901). We
know, for example, that Muir met and stayed with the pioneer Hale
Tharp in his one-log cabin at Crescent Meadow, and later witnessed a
forest fire while exploring the region near Tule River. Caught in the
midst of the fire, Muir "was glad of the opportunity presented to
study the methods of its destruction." Muir thought that for all the
destructiveness of the fire, it was nonetheless a natural and necessary
event, providing seedlings with the sunlight and free space essential
for survival. Even the smoldering forest floor Muir judged the more
beautiful as "the sun looked cheerily down the openings in the forest
floor, turning the black smoke to a beautiful brown, as if all was for
the best." Only when his mule was incapable of traveling further did
Muir quit the sequoia groves and descend west into the foothills of
the Tulare region.

   When Muir came down from the mountains, the scope of his
studies widened yet further. The infant agribusiness of California's
San Joaquin Valley surprisingly becomes a subject of his next letter
to the *Bulletin.* In "Tulare Levels" Muir gives a lesson on the "new
agriculture" of the region. He tells how the farmer is dependent on
the mountain for soil as well as water, thus connecting the farmers'
well-being and the welfare of business directly to the mountains.
Then, evidently still a little self-conscious about discussing farming,
he points out that "the agriculture of a country depends upon its
geology and climate, a fact which I state here for the purpose of
explaining my interest in farming. . . ." "Tulare Levels" can be seen
as a subdued rehearsal for his famous letter "God's First Temples—
How Shall We Preserve Them?" published early the following year in
the Sacramento *Record-Union.*[1] Muir was ready to assume a place in

   1. The letter to the *Union* may be found reprinted in Frederick R. Gunsky,
South of Yosemite (Garden City: Natural History Press, 1968), pp. 242–45; and
discussed in Robert Engberg, "John Muir: From Poetry to Politics, 1871–
1876," in *The World of John Muir,* ed. Lawrence R. Murphy and Dan Collins,
pp. 10–19. Another early attempt to influence public opinion is Muir's 1877

the human community, something he had for many years been loath to do.

Tulare Levels

When one comes suddenly out of the woods everything is novel. The wide arching sky, the flowing plains, fields, dogs, horses, oxen, are beheld as never seen before, and even our fellow-beings are regarded with something of the same keenness and freshness of perception that is brought to the study of a new species of wild animal. My first specimens of the perpendicular animal were a hearty, jovial company of lumbermen, redolent of pine gum, and as wholly unconventional as saw-logs. My next were found in a long string of dusty teamsters hauling lumber from the pines to the plains. These formed two well marked varieties, with distinguishing characteristics derived chiefly from the animals they drove, the one equine, the other bovine, both of which gave forcible illustration of the Scripture, "Dust thou art." At the base of the range I discovered a Rocky Mountain adventurer, whose free wild life was patent in every line and sign of his countenance, and a couple of bearish bear hunters, who lived and moved and had their being in bears.

JOLLY FARMERS

Lastly, out here in the smooth Tulare levels[2] I find a group of gentle grangers, that, taken all in all, are the most radiant and joyful set of farmers I have yet met in California. Every specimen is bright with smiles, and challenges congratulation like homebound prospectors who have "struck it rich." Most California farmers are afflicted with dry rot, which makes these

letter to the San Francisco *Real Estate Circular,* which called for a ban on all sheep grazing and timber cutting above 7,000 feet; it is reviewed in Engberg, "John Muir's 'Great Evils from Destruction of Forests,' " *Pacific Historian* 25 (Summer 1981): 10–14.

2. The Tulare region extends west from the Sierra foothills into the great San Joaquin plain of central California. Grangerville stood on the banks of the Kings River some fifty miles southeast of Fresno.

thrifty fellows all the more remarkable. It is now autumn, but their fields are yet full of spring. The generous soil seems unwilling to rest, and continues to pour forth its benedictions more lavishly than the most sanguine could anticipate. "Look," say these jubilant fellows, as they triumphantly showed me their wealth. "Look at that broom-corn, dense and impenetrable as canebreak," with panicles enough to sweep the State and "that Indian corn, grown after wheat, with ears so high you cannot reach them; and at these level sheets of alfalfa mowed, heaven knows how often. I tell you, sir, we have found it out; we want no better thing, no bigger bonanza. For the last ten years we have played at farming as at cards, speculating and gambling, scouring over thousand-acre lots with mustangs and gang-plows, and putting in crop after crop, that are in yet; but these dry games are played out. Two years ago we had wit enough to construct an irrigating ditch from King's river to Mussel Slough, big enough to moisten our half and quarter sections, and you see the result."

ALL ABOUT A DITCH

It appears, therefore, that all this physical and moral brightness flows directly from a ditch. The village itself, with its schoolhouse and church, has come out of the ditch. In the blocking out of the mountains by glaciers, and in their after-sculpture by torrents and avalanches, an immense quantity of detritus is carried to the lowlands, and it was in tracing these mountain chips that I was led into the Grangeville fields. The agriculture of a country depends upon its geology and climate, a fact which I state here for the purpose of explaining my interest in farming; besides it is hardly possible that wheat fields can ever be viewed with indifference by one who is often hungry. But to return to the ditch, I find that it is three feet deep and twenty-five feet wide at the bottom, and that the water flowed in it for the first time about the end of last April. It appears, therefore, that this grand agricultural revival was accomplished in six months—a fact that seems incredible on passing over the gray, arid plains out of which these green fields were made. In the application of the water it was found that the soil became thoroughly saturated for a distance of 200 yards or more on either side of the branch ditches, making it wholly unnecessary to overflow the fields. But so simple a method is not applicable everywhere. The soil of these Grangeville fields, and of a considerable portion of the plain between them and the foothills, is composed of a fine sandy loam, deposited by King's river floods in nearly level sheets like the leaves of a book. But the greater portion of the soils of the Sacramento, San Joaquin and Tulare valleys are of an entirely different origin, and the particles of which they are composed are put together in quite another way from those of the river deltas, so that to irrigate them it is found necessary to spread out the water in a sheet over the entire surface.

THE NEW AGRICULTURE

With reference to irrigation, all the lands of these valleys may be regarded as belonging to two distinct classes—the first comprehending all that are being degraded by atmospheric weathering; the second, all that are being elevated by deposition of fresh soil from extraordinary river floods. The so-called hog-wallow lands belong to the first, all the river bottoms to the second, each requiring different methods of irrigation. But farmers are coming to life, experiments are being made, and the problems connected with the watering of every kind of soil, are being persistently wrought out. The price of land in this vicinity has nearly quadrupled since the completion of the ditch, ranging now from about five to thirty dollars an acre. The greater number of the farmers here own shares in the ditch, and as long as snow falls on the mountains their water is sure. The price charged for the irrigation of fields belonging to outsiders is a dollar and a half per acre; and this Granger company in their first love are also offering settlers shares of water at prime cost. To farmers coming from the rainlands of the East it must seem hard to be obliged to buy not only land but water, as if the first comers had taken possession of the clouds. Nevertheless all seem satisfied with the necessities of the new agriculture on trial, every one to whom I have put the question, declaring that he would rather have a ditch than a cloud of his own. The question of water-rights in general is beset with great difficulties, many of the most important ditches being owned by companies, who refuse to sell a single share to farmers, thus forming conditions under which the maintenance of the true agricultural independence seems impossible. But notwithstanding "a'that and a'that" the thirsty ground is being watered, cheerless shanties, sifted through and through with dry winds, are being displaced by true homes embowered in trees and lovingly broidered with flowers; and contentment, which in California is perhaps the very rarest of the virtues, is now beginning to take root. Irriguous revivals are breaking out over all the glad plains, and wildcat farming is dead.

GRANGERVILLE,
OCTOBER 25, 1875

This book concludes with the short letter entitled "South Dome," published in the November 18, 1875, edition of the *Bulletin* and written when Muir had brought his season's travels full circle. In it Muir recounts the events which led to the building of a "stairway" to the top of "South Dome" (Yosemite's Half Dome) and playfully mocks those who consider mountains "conquered" when climbed. He remains optimistic that adding man to the list of creatures scrambling along the top of the Dome will not harm it in any way, although he recognizes that one result of bringing people into the mountains is to eliminate the "wild" from wilderness: "Now the pines will be carved with the initials of Smith and Jones, and the gardens strewn with tin cans and bottles, but the winter gales will blow most of this rubbish away . . ."

Muir closes with a hint of the vexing questions to face the next generation: How many wilderness visitors are too many? How might the wilderness be both visited and preserved? Ending this series of travels where he had begun them a season before—in his beloved Yosemite—Muir now holds the firm conviction that the destinies of humankind and mountains are intimately linked.

South Dome

The Yosemite South Dome[1] is the noblest rock in the Sierra, and George Anderson,[2] an indomitable Scotchman, has made a way to its summit. All the surface features of the flank of the range, "Domes," "conoids," "Mountains," "hills," and "rocks," are extremely simple in form and sculpture as compared with the jagged peaks marshaled along the summit, and the question of the accessibility of any one of them may be conclusively decided in a few hours, leaving no room whatever for

1. The famous Half Dome of Yosemite Valley.

2. Anderson was a Valley resident and part-time guide, and this article is the basis for almost all we know about him, other than that he constructed the trail from Happy Isles to Vernal Falls some years later, a business venture which evidently did not pay.

"South Dome, Liberty Cap and Nevada Fall, Yosemite." Snow's Hotel visible. Pencil drawing published by George Baker, San Francisco, 1870s. Courtesy the Bancroft Library.

the play of effort-making, or for those exciting hopes and fears so grateful to the strong mountaineer. With the exception of the conoidal summit of Mount Starr King, and a few minor spires and pinnacles, the South Dome is the only inaccessible rock of the valley, and its inaccessibility is pronounced in very severe and simple terms, leaving no trace of hope for the climber without artificial means. But longing eyes were none the less fixed on its noble brow, and the Anderson way will be eagerly ascended.

THE DOME DESCRIBED

The Dome rises from the level floor of the valley to the height of very nearly a mile. The north side is absolutely vertical from the summit to a depth of about 1,900 feet. On the south it is nearly vertical to as great a depth. The west side presents a very steep and firmly drawn curve from the summit down a thousand feet or more; while on the east, where it is united with the dividing ridge between the great Tenaya and Nevada canyons, the Dome may be easily approached within six or seven hundred feet of the summit, where it rises in a smooth, graceful curve just a few degrees too steep to climb. Nearly all Sierra rocks are accessible on the eastern or upper side, because the glacial force which eroded them out of the solid acted from this direction; but special conditions in the position and structure of the South Dome prevented the formation of the ordinary low grade, and it is this steep upper portion that the plucky Anderson has overcome. John Conway, a resident of the valley,[3] has a flock of small boys who climb smooth rocks like lizards, and some two years ago he sent them up the dome with a rope, hoping they might be able to fasten it with spikes driven into fissures, and thus reach the top. They took the rope in tow and succeeded in making it fast two or three hundred feet above the point ordinarily reached, but finding the upper portion of the curve impracticable without laboriously drilling into the rock, he called down his lizards, thinking himself fortunate in effecting a safe retreat.

3. Conway was granted the privilege of building toll roads in the Valley, and was responsible for completing the trail to Little Yosemite Valley and the "Four Mile Trail" to the summit of Glacier Point.

ANDERSON'S FEAT

Mr. Anderson began with Conway's old rope, part of which still remains in place, and resolutely drilled his way to the top, inserting eyebolts five or six feet apart, and making his rope fast to each in succession, resting his foot on the last bolt while he drilled for the next above. Occasionally some irregularity in the curve or slight foothold would enable him to climb fifteen or twenty feet independently of the rope, which he would pass and begin drilling again, the whole being accomplished in a few days. From this slender beginning he will now proceed to construct a substantial stairway which he hopes to complete in time for next year's travel; and as he is a man of rare energy the thing will surely be done. Then, all may sing "Excelsior" in perfect safety.

MR. MUIR TAKES A WALK UP THE SOUTH DOME

On my return to the valley the other day I immediately hastened to the Dome, not only for the pure pleasure climbing in view, but to see what else I might enjoy and learn. Our first winter storm had bloomed and all the mountains were mantled in fresh snow. I was therefore a little apprehensive of danger from the slipperyness of the rock, Anderson himself refusing to believe that any one could climb his rope in the condition it was then in. Moreover, the sky was overcast, and solemn snow-clouds began to curl and wreath themselves around the summit of the Dome, and my late experiences on icy Shasta came to mind.[4] But reflecting that I had matches in my pocket, and that a little firewood might be found, I concluded that in case of a dark storm the night could be spent on the Dome without suffering anything worth caring for. I therefore pushed up alone and gained the top without the slightest difficulty. My first view was perfectly glorious. A massive cloud of a pure pearl lustre was arched across the valley, from wall to wall, the one end resting upon El Capitan, the other on Cathedral Rocks, the brown meadows shadowed beneath, with short reaches of the river shimmering in changeful light. Then, as I stood on the tremen-

---

4. A reference to the near-fatal climb of Shasta, detailed in his December 2, 1874, letter to the *Evening Bulletin*.

ous verge overlooking Mirror Lake, a flock of smaller clouds, white as snow, came swiftly from the north, trailing over the dark forests, and arriving on the brink of the valley descended with god-like gestures through Indian Canyon and over the [Royal] Arches and North Dome, moving rapidly, yet with perfect deliberation. On they came, nearer, nearer, beneath by feet, gathering and massing, and filling the Tenaya abyss. Then the sun shone free, lighting them through and through and painting them with the splendors of the rainbow. It was one of those brooding days that come just between Indian summer and winter, when the clouds are like living creatures. Now and then the Valley appeared all bright and cloudless, with its crystal river meandering through colored meadow and grove, while to the eastward the snowy peaks rose in glorious array, keenly outlined on the pure azure. Then the clouds would come again, wreathing the Dome, and making a darkness like night.

VIEW FROM THE SUMMIT

Notwithstanding the enthusiastic eagerness of tourists to reach the summit of this Dome the general views of the valley from here are far less striking than those from many other points, chiefly because of the foreshortening effect produced by looking from so great a height. North Dome is dwarfed almost beyond recognition. The splendid sculpture of the arches is scarcely noticed and the walls on both sides seem comparatively low and sunken. The Dome itself is the most sublime feature of all Yosemite views, and that is beneath our feet. The view of Little Yosemite Valley is very fine, though inferior to one obtained from the base of Starr King; but the summit landscapes towards Mount Lyell, Dana and Conness are very effective and complete. When the sublime ice-floods of the glacial period poured down the flank of the range over what is now Yosemite Valley, they were compelled to break through a dam of domes extending across from Mount Starr King to North Dome; and as the period began to draw near a close and the ice currents shallowed and divided, South Dome was first to emerge from the icy waste, burnished and glowing like a crystal; and though it has sustained the wear and tear of the elements tens of thousands of

"Lake Starr King." Engraver unknown. In Muir, *The Mountains of California*, p. 119.

years, it yet remains not merely a monument but a history of the glaciers that brought it to light. Its entire surface is covered with glacial hieroglyphics whose interpretation is the great reward of all who devoutly study them.

BOTANY OF THE DOME

Before closing this letter I might say a word or two concerning the botany of the Dome. There are four clumps of pines growing in the summit representing three species, *Pinus flexilis, P. contorta* and *P. pondorosa—var. Jeffregii*—all three repressed and storm beaten. The Alpine spiraea grows here also, and blooms bonniely with potentilia, ivesia, erigeron, eriogonum, penstemon, solidago,[5] and four or five species of grasses and sedges, differing in no respect from those of other summits of the same elevation.

"CONQUERING" MOUNTAINS—YOSEMITE IN AUTUMN

I have always discouraged as much as possible every project for laddering the South Dome, believing it would be a fine thing to keep this garden untrodden. Now the pines will be carved with the initials of Smith and Jones, and the gardens strewn with tin cans and bottles, but the winter gales will blow most of this rubbish away, and avalanches may strip off the ladders; and then it is some satisfaction to feel assured that no lazy person will ever trample these gardens. When a mountain is climbed it is said to be conquered—as well say a man is conquered when a fly lights on his head. Blue jays have trodden the Dome many a day; so have beetles and chipmunks, and Tissiack will hardly be more conquered, now that man is added to her list of visitors. His louder scream and heavier scrambling will not stir a line of her countenance.

Yosemite Falls are flowing low these autumn days, so are streams of Yosemite travel, the one being a sure measure of the other. Nevertheless, at no time of the year is the valley more intensely lovely—the meadows frost-crystaled in the morning, sun-bathed in the warm noon; the oak leaves scarlet and brown,

5. These are Brewer's cinquefoil, mousetails, alpine asters, creogonum (?), pride of the mountain, and alpine goldenrod.

poplars and azaleas yellow; the Merced singing sweetly over low
pebbly bars; ouzels dipping along the margin; trout leaping in
sunny mirror-pools, the sheen of their scales blending with the
flashing water. Later, golden rods blooming along the banks;
violets and Johnsworts growing cheerily beneath withered
breckens, and all the mosses are rising from the dead.

YOSEMITE VALLEY,
NOVEMBER 10, 1875

"Near View of the Yo-Semite Falls, 2,500 Feet in Height." Engraved ca. 1860 by Thomas Armstrong from a photograph by C. L. Weed. In Hutchings, *Scenes of Wonder and Curiosity in California,* p. 113.

SELECTED SOURCES AND
LIST OF READINGS

Badè, William Frederic, ed. *The Life and Letters of John Muir.*
2 vols. Boston: Houghton Mifflin, 1923-24.

Brewer, William H. *Up and Down California in 1860-1864: The
Journal of William H. Brewer, Professor of Agriculture in the
Sheffield Scientific School from 1864 to 1903.* Edited by Francis P.
Farquhar. New Haven: Yale University Press, 1930. Reprint.
Berkeley: University of California Press, 1966.

Carr, Jeanne C. "John Muir." *The Californian* 1 (1890):88-94.

Cohen, Michael P. *The Pathless Way: John Muir and American
Wilderness* (Madison: University of Wisconsin Press, 1984).

Doran, Jennie Elliott. *A Bibliography of John Muir: With a Reference List to John Muir's Newspaper Articles by Cornelius Beach
Bradley.* San Francisco: Sierra Club, 1916. A complete listing of
Muir's letter-articles to the San Francisco *Daily Evening Bulletin* is
included.

Engberg, Robert. "John Muir's 'Great Evils from the Destruction of
Forests.'" *The Pacific Historian* 25:4 (Winter 1981): 10-14. (On a
rediscovered 1876 or 1877 letter to a San Francisco publication.)

Engberg, Robert, and Donald Wesling, eds. *John Muir To Yosemite
and Beyond: Writings from the Years 1863-1875.* Madison:
University of Wisconsin Press, 1980.

Fleck, Richard W. "John Muir's Evolving Attitudes toward Native
American Cultures." *American Indian Quarterly* 4:1 (February
1978):19-31.

Giles, Rosena A. *Shasta County California.* Oakland: Biobooks,
1949.

Gunsky, Frederic R., ed. *South of Yosemite: Selected Writings of
John Muir.* Garden City, N.Y.: Natural History Press, 1968.

Horn, Elizabeth L. *Wildflowers of the Sierra Nevada.* Beaverton,
Oreg.: Touchstone Press, 1976.

Hutchings, J. M. *Scenes of Wonder and Curiosity in California:
A Tourist's Guide to the Yo-Semite Valley.* New York and San
Francisco: A. Roman, 1871.

Interview with Elizabeth Marston (Mrs. William Frederic) Badè, San
  Diego, California, December 26, 1978.
Inventory of the John Muir Papers. Published by the Holt-Atherton
  Library, University of the Pacific, Stockton, California. Revised
  January–May 1976. The Papers are now undergoing new organiza-
  tion and microfilming.
John Muir Collection. Bancroft Library, University of California,
  Berkeley. A small collection of Muir letters mostly dating from the
  early 1900s, although a few from the 1870s are present.
John Muir Papers. Holt-Atherton Pacific Center for Western Studies,
  University of the Pacific, Stockton, California. The archives now
  contain the manuscripts previously held at Yosemite National Park.
  Muir's personal library of over 500 volumes has recently been
  added.
Kimes, William F., and Maymie B. Kimes. *John Muir: A Reading
  Bibliography.* Palo Alto: William P. Wrenden Books and Manu-
  scripts, 1978. The most recent bibliography.
King, Clarence. *Mountaineering in the Sierra Nevada.* Boston: James
  R. Osgood and Company, 1872. Reprint. Lincoln: University of
  Nebraska Press, 1970.
Kneeland, Samuel. *The Wonders of the Yosemite Valley and of
  California.* Boston, 1872.
Limbaugh, Ronald H., et al., eds. "John Muir Newsletter." Holt-
  Atherton Pacific Center for Western Studies, University of the
  Pacific, Stockton, California. An ongoing newsletter for persons
  interested in Muir's life.
Matthes, François E. *The Incomparable Valley: A Geologic Inter-
  pretation of the Yosemite.* Edited by Fritiof Fryxell. Berkeley and
  Los Angeles: University of California Press, 1950.
Muir, John. "The Ancient Glaciers of the Sierra." *The Californian*
  2 (1880):550–61.
Muir, John. *Letters to a Friend: Written to Mrs. Ezra S. Carr, 1866–
  1879.* Edited by William Frederic Badè. Boston: Houghton Mifflin,
  1915. Reprint. Dunwoody, Ga.: Norman S. Berg, 1973.
Muir, John. Letters to the San Francisco *Daily Evening Bulletin,*
  October 29, 1874, to November 18, 1875. A complete set of the
  newspapers may be found in the Bancroft Library, Berkeley, Cali-
  fornia; copies of several of the articles are in the John Muir Papers
  (Stockton, California), with Muir's revisions appearing in marginal
  notes.
Muir, John. *The Mountains of California.* New York: Century, 1894.
  Reprint. Dunwoody, Ga.: Norman S. Berg, n.d. The 1911 edition

and the reprint contain a map showing most of the places Muir visited in 1874–75.

Muir, John, ed. *Picturesque California and the Region West of the Rocky Mountains from Alaska to Mexico.* San Francisco and New York: J. Dewing Company, 1888.

Muir, John. *Steep Trails.* Edited by William Frederic Badè. Boston: Houghton Mifflin, 1918.

Muir, John. *The Story of My Boyhood and Youth.* Boston: Atlantic Monthly, 1913. Reprint. Madison: University of Wisconsin Press, 1965.

Muir, John. *The Yosemite.* New York: Century, 1912.

Murphy, Lawrence R., and Dan Collins, eds. *The World of John Muir.* Stockton: University of the Pacific for the Holt-Atherton Pacific Center for Western Studies, 1981. A collection of essays about Muir.

Nordhoff, Charles. *California for Health, Pleasure and Residence.* New York: Harper and Brothers, 1872.

Olmsted, R. R., Ed. *Scenes of Wonder & Curiosity from Hutchings' California Magazine 1856–1861.* Berkeley: Howell-North, 1962.

Sargent, Shirley. *John Muir in Yosemite.* Yosemite, Calif.: Flying Spur Press, 1971. The delightful popular account of his Yosemite years.

Southern, May. "May Southern Notebook." Binder no. 6. Original manuscript at Shasta State Historic Park, Shasta, California. Memoirs of a Shasta pioneer.

Stone, Livingston. "Report of the Operations During 1872 at the United States Salmon-Hatchery Establishment on the McCloud River." *U.S. Commission of Fish and Fisheries,* part 2, *Report of the Commissioner.* Washington: Government Printing Office, 1874. Pp. 168–215.

Teale, Edwin Way, ed. *The Wilderness World of John Muir.* Boston: Houghton Mifflin, 1954. A fine collection of Muir's best-known works.

Webster, Paul, and the editors of "The American West." *The Mighty Sierra.* Palo Alto: American West Publishing Company, 1971.

Whitney, Josiah D. *The Yosemite Guide Book.* (Published by Authority of the [California] State Legislature.) Cambridge: Cambridge University Press, 1870.

Whitney, Steven. *A Sierra Club Naturalist's Guide: The Sierra Nevada.* San Francisco: Sierra Club Books, 1979. An outstanding guidebook to the Sierra's life zones, animals, and plants.

Wolfe, Linnie Marsh, ed. *John of the Mountains: The Unpublished Journals of John Muir.* Boston: Houghton Mifflin, 1938. Reprint. Madison: University of Wisconsin Press, 1979.

Wolfe, Linnie Marsh, ed. *Son of the Wilderness: The Life of John Muir.* New York: Knopf, 1945. Reprint. Madison: University of Wisconsin Press, 1978. The biography.

INDEX

COMPOSED BY THE COMPOSING ROOM, KIMBERLY, WISCONSIN
MANUFACTURED BY FAIRFIELD GRAPHICS, FAIRFIELD, PENNSYLVANIA
TEXT AND DISPLAY LINES ARE SET IN TIMES ROMAN

Library of Congress Cataloging in Publication Data
Muir, John, 1838–1914.
John Muir summering in the Sierra.
"Articles written by John Muir for the San Francisco
Daily evening bulletin in the years 1874–1875"—Pref.
Bibliography: p.
Includes index.
1. Natural history—California—Addresses, essays,
lectures. 2. Natural history—Sierra Nevada Mountains
(Calif. and Nev.)—Addresses, essays, lectures.
3. Muir, John, 1838–1914—Addresses, essays, lectures.
4. Naturalists—United States—Biography—Addresses,
essays, lectures. I. Engberg, Robert, 1943–
II. Title.
QH105.C2M797 1984   508.794′4   83-16918
ISBN 0-299-09620-3
ISBN 0-299-09624-6 (pbk.)